RUNNING YOUR
BUSINESS SUCCESSFULLY

Also by Peg Moran

INVEST IN YOURSELF

Running Your Business Successfully

A WOMAN'S GUIDE
TO SURVIVING THE FIRST TWO YEARS

PEG MORAN

Doubleday & Company, Inc., Garden City, New York
1985

Library of Congress Cataloging in Publication Data

Moran, Peg.
  Running your business successfully.

    1. New business enterprises—United States—Handbooks,
manuals, etc.   2. Women-owned business enterprises—
United States—Handbooks, manuals, etc.   I. Title.
HD62.5.M674   1985   658.1'1'024042   84-4102
ISBN 0-385-18799-8

To all of us who are striving
to make a dream come true

Acknowledgments

This book is an accumulation of practical knowledge gained from many people over many years. My special thanks to

- —My son John, who introduced his reluctant mom to the exciting new world of computers.
- —Michael Phillips for sharing with me the Briarpatch Marketing Plan.
- —Bill Bell and Sally Shepard for help with the chapter on advertising and promotion.
- —Mike McKeever for suggesting changes in the "Money" chapter of this book.
- —Pat Loomis for her fine work on the interviews.
- —Jim Howland and Elaine Dechter for their assistance with the manuscript.
- —Susan Schwartz of Doubleday and Al Zuckerman of Writers House—new friends and business associates.

Contents

Introduction

Welcome to the world of women entrepreneurs. It's a wonderful and sometimes frustrating world of too much to do and too little time to do it. Lots of bills and not enough money to pay them. A world of Eric, your three-year-old son, eating poinsettia leaves just before your scheduled departure for a meeting with your banker.

I know this world well. I've been a part of it for eleven years.

My first adventure in business was a small retail decorating shop in Petaluma, California. It never made me rich, but it did keep food on the table and a roof over my head. It also gave me time for baseball games and swimming lessons with my young son.

Upstream Press, a small publishing company, is my second business venture. Dedicated to helping women entrepreneurs, the company published *Invest in Yourself: A Woman's Guide to Starting Her Own Business* in 1982. Since then, Doubleday has taken over publication rights and commissioned this new book.

Why a workbook on the first two years in business? Simple. The first two years are the hardest, the longest, the most discouraging. During those first two years you will come across every business lesson there is to learn. Pricing. Marketing. Dealing with bankers and suppliers. Time management. Family conflicts. Role reversals. You'll come across all of these—and more.

Why a workbook that gives almost a third of its space to discussions of the personal side of business? Isn't it sufficient to know how to manipulate cash flow charts, balance statements, and other precisely measurable aspects of business? It's not.

What's just as important, and unfortunately usually ignored, is the people part of business. How we work. Why we work. What we need *as people* to keep us contributing to our businesses through thick and thin. This is just as much the core of any successful business as the mechanical manipulation of facts and figures.

Some of you may be more comfortable with the traditional material in Parts Two and Three. Skip Part One if you wish. But if you get stuck, bored, or discouraged, do the Part One chapters. You may find just the help you need.

Peg Moran
Rohnert Park, California
April 1984

RUNNING YOUR BUSINESS SUCCESSFULLY

PART ONE

THE PERSONAL SIDE OF BUSINESS

1

Mountains and Chuckholes

Most business books are long on the *business* side of business and very short on the *personal* side of business. I think that's a big mistake. Learning how to deal with feeling overwhelmed or isolated is just as important as learning how to deal with overdue accounts receivable or a delivery of damaged stock.

Take time to get to know yourself better as a business person. How do you set goals? Make decisions? Congratulate yourself? Settle problems?

Remember, YOU are your most important business asset. The more you learn about that asset the more you will be able to put it to use in your business. Let's look first at how you deal with the ups and downs of business cycles.

My business road is rarely straight and level. It seems I am either climbing a mountain or clambering, bruised, out of a chuckhole.

Mountain roads are business times when I'm working hard and everything is going right. Well-thought-out business plans are on course. No unexpected expenses pop up. Sales are smooth and steady.

It takes time and energy to climb mountains but the view from the top makes it all worth while. I feel great when business plans work as expected.

But when they don't? That's a chuckhole.

Some chuckholes are small and I can get around them easily. A slight readjustment is all it takes. Other chuckholes are gaping pits. The whole road has disappeared. They call for major rethinking and a new direction.

The first two years of Upstream Press were the typical mix of mountains and chuckholes.

I was climbing a mountain from the day I started writing *Invest in Yourself.* It was a busy, exciting time from June to December 1, 1981. Writing each morning. Interviewing other women in business. Getting estimates from typesetters and printers—and money from bankers. Swimming each afternoon to get the day's kinks out of my neck and shoulders.

Another, more strenuous mountain climb began in January 1982. I shifted gears from *writing* a book to *marketing* a book. With the help of two business associates, I launched our sales effort. Within weeks, two major chuckholes appeared. An expensive ad produced no sales. Not one! A small business convention organization that would have handled some of our sales went bankrupt. Another disaster!

It was time to retrench, rethink, and redo our market plan. We gradually made progress but it took much longer than expected. Too long for my associates. By August they wanted out. For me, their departure was another chuckhole.

I guess the most important lesson I've learned during these early years is not to be too enthralled by the mountaintops or too discouraged by the chuckholes. Each is a part of business life. I try to remind myself often that the road to success is always under construction.

Take some time to review your own business history. When were the peak times when you felt as though you were standing on a mountaintop? What chuckholes have you survived?

***Yours to Do.* I have been in business for _____ (months/years). These business experiences were mountain peaks for me.**

_____

_____

_____

_____

These were minor chuckholes. _____

_____

_____

_____

These chuckholes were so deep I thought I'd never climb out. _____

_____

_____

_____

And this is how I did. _____

_____

_____

_____

2
Fast Lane, Middle Lane, Slow Lane

I love excitement and challenge. But I want them in doses that suit *me.*

I like to zip into the fast lane once in a while—a business trip to New York, a presentation to two hundred women in Sacramento, a phone radio interview to Anywhere, U.S.A. But don't make me stay in the fast lane for long or I will burn out.

Most of my life I live in the middle or slow lane. My favorite recipe for a rewarding workday is to mix something mental with something physical. That's especially true when I'm writing.

Planting Corsican mint and writing a chapter is a good mix. So is building fences and making phone calls. A variety of activities keeps me sane, sensible, calmed down, and productive.

We hear a lot about burnout in public service jobs. Watch out for signs of burn out in you, the entrepreneur. Public service burnout seems to come from underload—not enough excitement and challenge. Too much repetition. Result: boredom and frustration.

Entrepreneurial burnout seems to come more from overload. Too many things to do. Too little time. Too many details all needing attention right now. Result: exhaustion.

Learn about your natural pace. And use it in your business. Maybe you are an early riser and work best in the morning. Schedule your most important work for that time of the day. Maybe, like me, you hate to get up in the morning and work best after 10 A.M.

What about your social needs? Some of us need to see lots of people or we feel lonely or neglected. Others prefer to work alone. Some are content to deal with abstract planning. And some need to be busy with details.

Your personal style can work well in your business. That, to me, is one of the joys of being my own boss. I can make the work fit me. If I work for someone else, I will have to fit the work.

Here are some questions to help you discover your natural pace and working style. Are you using them in your business?

Yours to Do. I like to get up at _____ A.M. I like to go to bed at ___ P.M. I find that I work best between _____ and _____ o'clock. I like to see _____ (number) people a day. It's especially important for me to keep in touch with these people. _____

_____

_____

How important are physical activities to me? _____

_____

Am I mixing enough physical activity into my business life?_____ If I'm not, how can I?_____

_____

_____

My natural pace is to live these percentages of my life in each lane.

> _____% fast lane
>
> _____% middle lane
>
> _____% slow lane

I feel my current business pace is just right or needs to be changed.

_____

These are the changes I want to make. _____

_____

_____

I want each business day to be satisfying. This is the one most important thing I have to do each day to feel a sense of accomplishment each evening. _____

_____

3
Memos to Me

Being my own boss, I don't have a supervisor to tell me I'm doing a great job. And yet I have a very human need to be appreciated. Without a boss to give me appreciation, I've had to invent other ways to get it.

Sometimes I have silent conversations between two parts of myself— the shy retiring little girl who wants to be appreciated and the outgoing, confident adult who is comfortable giving congratulations. Sometimes I put a memo to myself in my workbasket: "Good piece of work on those projections." Sometimes I write a note reminding me to call a friend, tell her some good news, and bask in the warmth of her esteem. Sometimes I reread an entry in my journal that details the horrors of a past business day, knowing that that particular problem is now solved.

Giving appreciation to myself is great practice. Knowing how much I need and relish it, I am better at recognizing the same need in others. Employees and subcontractors need to hear they've done a good job. Children need to hear loving reminders of their progress. Husbands need to hear your appreciation of their support.

Written forms of appreciation seem especially important. A thank-you note when a supplier's bookkeeper straightens out the account. A note to the radio station saying this week's spot is really bringing in the customers. Each takes only a minute to write, and twenty cents to send. Just think how you'd feel getting a note like this. You'll send a lot more!

Yours to Do. These are memos of appreciation I want to send myself.

_____

_____

_____

_____

_____

These are people I can call to share good news. They will appreciate

what I've done! _____

_____

_____

_____

These are other people to whom I want to express my appreciation. And the reason I appreciate them. _____

_____

_____

_____

_____

_____

I'll tell them in person or write them a note within the week.

4
Notes to the C.E.O.

I am generally an optimistic, positive person. I usually don't worry very much. But last spring I did.

My business associate was taking a vacation with her husband in Mexico. I was left to manage things alone for a week. It was a critical business time. We had revamped our Upstream Press market plan after some initial disasters and it was slowly taking hold. But money was running low. New funds were imperative. For the first time since the beginning of the project I was really worried.

Instead of sleeping soundly, as I usually do, I tossed and turned, reviewing the day's frustrations. I was wearing myself out with anxiety. One night, as I tried to relax, a picture formed in my mind. This is what I saw.

> Dressed in pj's, I'm sitting beside a huge carved door. A shiny brass plate on the door says: CHIEF EXECUTIVE OFFICER. The door is closed but a slit of light, about an inch wide, appears along the bottom.
>
> Clipboard on my knees, I'm thoughtfully rubbing the eraser end of a pencil along my eyebrow. Then I write a note on the clipboard pad, tear it off, and shove it under the door. The note reads, "Horrid day today."

I watched myself recap the whole day's activities with notes and shove them under the door. "Chris on vacation. I miss her." "Saw banker. No luck." "Need help."

Each night during the crisis I used the same visualization. I'd go about my day's work as planned. At night I'd report the results to the C.E.O. I found my worry quickly disappeared, replaced by my usual buoyant good spirits.

Some nights I visualized my notes returned with words of encouragement. "Keep it up." "You're on the right track." One night I received a specific suggestion. I wrote, "Money situation still critical. Any ideas?" The answer came back, "Try real estate."

The answer didn't make any sense but the next day I called my realtor. And, sure enough, he came up with a suggestion that eventually did solve the money crunch.

What happened with this visualization? I really don't know. Maybe I found a way to tap into my unconscious. Maybe the God of my childhood answered some prayers.

I do know that it helped me to stop worrying. Instead of scattering my energy with worry, I was able to concentrate my energy to solve the problem.

Yours to Do. **I worry most about** _____

_____

These are ways that I scatter my energy when I worry. _____

_____

_____

These are ways that I help myself to stop worrying. _____

_____

_____

_____

This is my own special antiworry visualization. I will use it next time I get myself into an anxious state. _____

_____

_____

_____

_____

5

On the Road . . .
to Where?

I find the whole subject of goal setting fascinating. Just how do we decide where we want to go? And having decided, just how do we get to our destination?

I find that I have two different ways of setting and achieving goals. One method is very linear, very rational. The other is more emotional and intuitive.

The rational method is easier to explain. I first look at my life as it is right now. Then I decide what I like and don't like about it. I choose what I want to keep and what I want to get rid of. Next I state my goals in firm, positive statements. At this point I have a plan of action to follow.

Then comes the hard part—following that plan. I try, at all times, to act according to my plan. When I don't, my goal statement reminds me of the fact. It becomes an alert siren that I am off course.

There is one last, very important step. Each week I keep a written record of how well I've followed my plan. I never record the times during the week I've failed. I concentrate *only* on times I've succeeded.

I used this system to set and achieve a goal of weekly exercise. First, I looked at my life. No exercise on a regular basis. Next, I decided I didn't like not exercising. I wanted to exercise regularly. So I created a goal statement: I am exercising vigorously three times a week.

If I didn't exercise by the middle of the week, my goal statement nagged at me. Each Friday I wrote details of how I actually accomplished my goal. Those reports gave me a history of successfully accomplishing my goal.

In January I joined an aerobic dance class. I noted in my journal, "Exercise class, now I never did think of that as a solution. I love it! Dancing twice a week is more exercise than tennis three times a week." I still continue to exercise regularly. Now it's a habit that is firmly fixed as part of my life.

My second goal-setting system is much less rational. More emotional and intuitive. And more difficult to explain. It starts with my trying to imagine how it would *feel* to be doing something.

Eleven years ago I pictured myself as an interior decorator—and liked it. More recently I pictured myself as an author/publisher—and the image fit.

Each affirmative response was the beginning of a business vision. I added more details by asking more questions. How will this image of me as a decorator carry out her business? Will she have a large shop or a small one? What kinds of clients will come in? What kinds of fabrics does she want to carry in the shop? What wallpapers fit the image? Is manufacturing part of the picture?

Will that author feel most comfortable writing by hand or with a typewriter? Or word processor? Will publicizing the book be comfortable or uncomfortable? Will television be intimidating? Will selling rights to a major publisher add or subtract from the vision? Little by little, by answering such questions, I created a very detailed picture of the businesses I wanted to run.

The next step was to bring that vision gradually into reality. But I continued to make adjustments to my dream as I went along. I never hesitated to add new information as it became available or subtract parts that didn't fit anymore. In other words, the building process was never static.

In a very real sense I feel as though I am living inside of my goal/vision. I perfect it day by day. Daily business tasks are like daily housekeeping. They keep my vision bright and shiny.

This intuitive way of achieving goals also answers two objections I've always had to rational goal-setting systems. How to handle new information? How to deal with detours?

Rational goal setters seem to ignore new information. That seems like a terrible waste. They also avoid detours. And detours have always intrigued me.

I appreciate new information. I can always use it to refine my vision. Instead of ignoring it as a distraction, I welcome new material for my building process.

And since I live inside my business goal/vision, there is no such thing as a detour! All that I am doing is—in one way or another—adding to my vision.

I was delighted one day to receive a phone call from London. A company in England wanted to purchase publication rights to my first book, *Invest in Yourself.* That phone call was the result of a "detour" I took almost a year previously—giving a ride to two British women at a booksellers' convention.

No matter how you do it—rationally or intuitively—it's important to find a way to think or feel your way into the future. It's equally important to remember that you are creating tomorrow today. Add two bricks to your house of business daily and you'll have a strong structure in five years. Neglect it today, it will fall down tomorrow.

Yours to Do. **This is my usual way of setting goals.** _____

_____

I am most comfortable setting goals rationally/intuitively. (Circle one.)

This is my image of me as a businesswoman. _____

_____

_____

This is my vision of my business. _____

_____

_____

_____

This is new information I have recently found that I can put to use in my business. _____

_____

This is an example of a detour that I'm sure was a detour. _____

_____

This is an example of a detour that turned out *not* to be a detour!

_____

6

Decisions: Found and Made

I have never been formally trained in business. Maybe that is why I am willing to trust my intuition as well as my intellect when searching for answers to business problems. Sometimes I pick over a problem, analyze its parts, and make a decision. Sometimes I find the answer by intuition. The answer is suddenly there. It's obvious. It's comfortable.

I *found* the decision to write my first book, *Invest in Yourself.* I woke up one morning and the idea was crystal clear—the audience, the divisions, even some chapter titles. I *made* decisions about the details—type style, size, number of interviews.

This is the way it seems to work for me. I find the large decisions in my life; and I make the small ones.

Each of us has her own style of making/finding decisions. And we usually shift fairly comfortably from intellect to intuition and back again in our personal lives. But, in business, people have the mistaken opinion that reason is the only faculty to use. It's not!

A strongly felt, intuitive reaction to a business situation is just as powerful. It's also a bit scary. For one thing, you can't explain it. And business associates usually want reasons—one, two, three.

Try combining both methods of decision making. In other words, when you hear an intuitive answer to a business question listen carefully. In the background you will probably also hear the supporting rational evidence. On the other hand, when you *make* an important decision, don't ignore any intuitive nudges, for or against.

Yours to Do. **This is an example of a business decision I *made*.**

_____

_____

This is an example of a business decision I *found*.

_____

_____

This is an example of a time when I should have trusted my intuition and didn't. _____

_____

This is an example of trusting my intuition in a business situation. Everyone thought I was crazy! I wasn't. _____

_____

_____

Here is an example of how I combined intuition and reason in a business decision. _____

_____

_____

7
Living in the World of Shoulds and Oughts

In our world of changing values I find a lot of *shoulds* and *oughts.* A son says, "Mom, you should have picked me up after the game this afternoon." Daughter says, "Mom, you ought to be here when I get home from school." Husband says, "You must come on that business trip to Chicago. You have to take an interest in my career."

I have a strong negative reaction to sentences that include *should, ought, must,* and *have to.* These words emphasize expectations about a role I play and camouflage real messages of honest needs and feelings.

What did your son really mean by saying you should have picked him up? Does the role of motherhood necessarily include car pooling? Or was the real message, "Mom, I'm feeling neglected," or "Mom, I really wanted you to see me hit that home run in the ninth inning"?

Peeling through those shoulds and oughts and getting to honest needs and feelings takes patience. And time to talk and listen.

As women of the eighties and as businesswomen, we hear a lot of shoulds and oughts. Some are blatant and some are very subtle. Whenever I hear one, I pinpoint the speaker. It helps me separate the person I am from roles others expect me to play.

Yours to Do. **Many times people talk to us, but not out loud. We hear them all the time, however, telling us that we *should* do this. We *ought* to be like that. Who's talking to you?**

"To be a better person, I should . . ."   **Says who?**

1. _____   _____

2. _____   _____

3. _____   _____

4. _____   _____

5. _____   _____

6. _____   _____

7. _____   _____

8. _____   _____

9. _____   _____

10. _____   _____

"To be a better businesswoman, I should . . ."   **Says who?**

1. _____   _____

2. _____   _____

3. _____   _____

4. _____   _____

5. _____   _____

6. _____   _____

7. _____   _____

8. _____   _____

9. _____   _____

10. _____   _____

8

My Business Experts

Through the years I have gathered around me wonderful business experts. Some of my experts have definite, official roles in my business—my banker, attorney, and accountant, for example. I selected them, not only for expertise in their chosen fields but also for their personalities. We think alike—or almost alike. I like them as people.

But that's only the beginning of my list of experts. I have others, less official, who are just as important. Let me tell you about four of them: Jean the Just, Fred the Falcon, Tom the Gabber, and Mother Murphy.

Jean the Just is my expert on positive attitude. She always has a good word about the world and everybody in it. Jean helps me see the brighter side of any situation. Coffee or lunch with her is a time for good humor and encouragement. Jean is an energetic businesswoman, supervising twenty-five members of her Mary Kay cosmetics team, but she is never too busy to return a phone call or write a cheery note. I can always count on Jean the Just.

Fred the Falcon is my "hardheaded businessman" expert. He sees liabilities in people and situations that I never see—personality conflicts, future problems, negative consequences. His opinions are stark and blunt, but he gives them only when asked. Otherwise he watches, in a rather bemused fashion, as I do business my own way. If I need to analyze the worst that could possibly happen, I call on Fred the Falcon.

Tom the Gabber is my "big picture" expert. If I want to talk about the economy in the year 2000, Tom is my man. Over a glass of wine and a good dinner we can talk for hours about the future of entrepreneurs, the financial impact of the price of oil, or the latest interesting articles in half a dozen different business magazines. Tom tends to scribble notes on paper napkins or yellow legal sheets. I have a collection of these bits of business wisdom tucked away in my files.

Mother Murphy is my refuge during a crisis in self-confidence. She'll feed me milk and cookies—or a cup of steaming tea—and listen to my tales of inadequacy. I sat on her porch one spring day and shook, overwhelmed by my commitment to write a book. Being an artist, Mother Murphy knows how hard it is to get paint on canvas or words on paper.

I might see my banker, accountant, or lawyer once a year. I keep much closer contact with my other experts. They are on constant call to help me be the best possible businesswoman I can be.

We all need these unofficial experts. Who are yours?

Yours to Do. These are my unofficial business experts. This is how they help me in my business.

_____

_____

_____

_____

_____

_____

_____

_____

_____

9
Time In and Time Out

I find one of the best things I can do for my business is take a vacation. I park my business problems, set them aside for several hours or several days, and explore other aspects of the world. I come back to my desk refreshed and bubbling with new ideas.

That is, I always come back refreshed *if* I take the time to get away. But I always seem to need vacations at the very busiest times. Awkward and unloyal for me to want a vacation when my business needs me most!

March 1982 was one of those times. I keep a journal so I can tell you exactly how I felt then.

. . . I feel really stressed, really tired, really not wanting to do anything at all. In fact, I would like to do *absolutely* nothing.

And then the "if onlys" come up.

— *If only* the money situation was settled.
— *If only* the market situation was clearer.
— *If only* I could see the light at the end of the tunnel.
— *If only* I didn't have such a back-breaking schedule.
— *If only* I could trust that others were really doing what should be done.
— *IF ONLY* I COULD GET AWAY FOR A VACATION!

I probably didn't get away for that needed break. I probably stuck it out and muddled through. But I'm gradually learning that it's most important to stop when it's hardest to stop.

No business problem is insurmountable but fatigue and frustration can block your vision of ways to overcome it. That's the exact time you need a new point of view. And a vacation gives it to you.

A total-care week at a Caribbean Club Med might be ideal but financially out of the question. How about an afternoon tennis game or a picnic with the kids? When was the last time you took a vacation?

Yours to Do. This is the last time I took a vacation. _____

When I left on vacation I felt _____

When I got back from vacation I felt _____

_____

This is a description of my ideal vacation! _____

_____

_____

_____

If I start to plan my finances and business schedule right now, I can take that vacation in _____
In the meantime I'll take mini-vacations. These are ten things I really enjoy doing. The next time I feel overwhelmed and need a break from business, I'll do one of them.

_____

_____

_____

_____

_____

_____

_____

_____

_____

_____

_____

_____

10
My Ideal Business

A couple of weeks ago I spent two hours with a woman while she worked through her confusion about how she wants to run her business. Jan is a tall, talented woman who dances, waits tables, and manufactures sheepskin clothing. She is thinking of devoting more time to manufacturing and less time to supplementing her income with restaurant work.

We talked for a while about the detail problems—expanding a seasonal product line, exploring new markets, evening out cash flow. We came up with some good ideas but I could see from Jan's face that she wasn't satisfied. We were dealing well with details but ignoring the larger picture. I asked her, "What would your ideal business look like?"

Jan took a sip of tea, stretched out her long legs, clasped her hands behind her head, and began to describe it. "I want to work four or five hours a day. I want to earn enough money to live comfortably. I want to dance every day in aerobics class. I want time for my friends—they're important to me. I *don't* want to be involved in selling. I want to work on a regular schedule year round instead of being jammed up right before Christmas." Then she leaned forward and said, "But I can't have a business like that! My father ran a small business for years. He says you can't get anywhere unless you work fifty or sixty hours a week."

It was obvious to both of us that Jan had absorbed a lot of messages about business from her father. She needs to separate her ideas about business from her father's. Until she does, Jan will be in a push/pull situation. Pushed by her own ideas of success. Pulled by her father's.

There are many different ways to do business. His way. Her way. My way. Your way. Each is just as valuable as any other.

I don't feel as though there is any *right* way to do business. To want to stay small is just great. To do business out of your home is not demeaning. It makes good business sense in some cases.

To want to work only five hours a day. To feel comfortable with a minimal income. To hand off selling to someone else. To hate deadlines. These are all legitimate factors to consider in business planning. So are family vacation schedules, Little League games, and upset tummies.

We live in a culture that emphasizes money and de-emphasizes personal worth. Our culture defines success as being bigger and more aggressive than the competition. War is hell. And so is business to a lot of people.

Business doesn't have to be conducted like a war—with winners and losers. It can be conducted so that everybody wins—me, my clients, my community. I can grow and prosper both personally and monetarily from conducting my business as it best suits me. When I treat myself with respect and understanding I can give both to my clients. I treat them not as numbers contributing to my cash flow and depleting my inventory but as the interesting, wonderful people they are.

And if enough of us conduct business with a high regard for our own needs and the needs of those around us—how can our town or city fail to benefit? We are contributing responsibly to our communities with goods, services, and human values.

It all starts with you and your willingness to listen to yourself. Structure your business in human terms and it will work not only for you but for the world around you.

Yours to Do. Okay, I'm willing to take a look at how I really want to run my business. It may seem totally unrealistic, but I'll take a look.

I want to work _____ hours a day.

I want to work only between _____ and _____ and be finished work by _____ o'clock.

I want to feel this way at the end of a business day. _____
_____

I want to see an average of _____ clients a day.

I also want to see an average of _____ social contacts a day.

In the morning I want to start my day with _____
_____

Then I'll _____
_____

By noon I'll have these things finished _____
_____
_____

In the afternoon I'll do this _____

and this _____

and this _____

In the evening I'll be free to _____
_____

This schedule gives me the business pace I want.

To refresh myself, I'll take vacations. I've planned a big one for

_____

And I'm making all the arrangements now to do it. In the meantime, when I get bored, restless, or irritable, I'll take mini-vacations by __

_____

To give myself the appreciation I deserve I'll do this. _____

_____

_____

And when I get worried I'll do this. _____

_____

I'll use this vision of me as a businesswoman to help me decide the details of my business. _____

_____

And when the going gets rough, this is the one most important concept I don't want to forget. _____

_____

I'm a good decision maker when I trust myself. Remember when __

_____ **!!!!**

I have listened to other people in the past when they've told me that in order to be a better businesswoman I should _____

_____ .

I heard this message from _____ .

The big question is, "Is that me?"

I've got these wonderful business experts around me.

_____

_____

_____

_____

And we can discuss how I can decrease these business activities I don't like. _____

_____

_____

And increase these activities I do like. _____

_____

_____

I'll tell them these are the reasons I find my business really satisfy-ing. _____

_____

_____

And these are the reasons I'm dissatisfied. _____

_____

_____

I'll tell my business experts this is how my ideal business looks to me. _____

_____

_____

_____

_____

_____

And that this is what "successful" means to me. _____

_____

_____

_____

I want to remind myself often that these are the major contributions I want to give:

To myself _____

_____

To my clients _____

_____

To my community _____

_____

PART TWO
TIME AND MONEY

11
Time

In Part One you examined your primary business asset—yourself. Now let's research your use of two other assets—time and money.

There are 168 hours in each week. Over the years I have created these guidelines to help make good use of that time.

1. I plan.
2. I set priorities.
3. I concentrate on the present task.
4. I don't let myself get frazzled by worry or exhausted by overwork.
5. I take time off.
6. I keep my office organization simple.
7. I write everything down.
8. I hand off work to other people.

Most small business owners consider an hour wasted if it's spent planning. Wrong! Any business person needs *at least* an hour a week to plan the next week's activities. And comparable time monthly, quarterly, and annually. In the early stages of Upstream Press we spent four hours each Friday afternoon planning the next week's tasks. That time was never wasted. It kept the company on course and the owners sane.

Yours to Do. **How much time do I currently devote to planning?**

_____

This is a schedule of the time I want to devote exclusively to planning.

Weekly _____

Monthly _____

Quarterly _____

Annually _____

Planning and setting priorities go together. When we plan we decide what we want to do. When we set priorities we choose what we want to do first, second, third. Before I started this book I planned out the whole project—titles of chapters, approximate word count, business owners to interview. Then I set my work priorities—a chapter completed each week-day. So, "Chapter on Time Management" appears at the top of today's list of my Six Most Important Things to Do. Other items on the list include:

> Mail Napa class list to Judy
> Call Pat regarding interviews
> Pick up notebook from Jean
> Appointment with accountant, 3 P.M.
> Pick up cat's medicine from vet

Writing yourself such a daily reminder is a great time management tool. It helps you both plan and set priorities. Do it after you finish a day's work or first thing in the morning before you start.

Discipline your choices. Don't expand the list to ten or twelve items. If you do, you are avoiding making decisions about more or less important tasks.

Don't defeat yourself by overscheduling your time. Any business day is cluttered with the unexpected. If you schedule only 30% of your time, the other 70% remains available for today's happenings.

Yours to Do. Here's my Six Most Important Things to Do list for to-morrow.

_____

_____

_____

_____

_____

_____

The Six Most Important Things to Do list works equally well for weekly, monthly, quarterly, and annual planning.

Yours to Do. These are the Six Most Important Things to Do during the next month.

_____

_____

_____

_____

_____

_____

These are the Six Most Important Things to Do during the year.

_____

_____

_____

_____

_____

_____

Concentration, for me, is the essence of time management. I clear my mind of distractions and work only at the task at hand. If I'm paying bills I concentrate on writing the checks correctly—not on next month's sales or book orders that need to be processed. When my mind does wander to a phone call I forgot to make on an oil change I need to arrange, I use slips of paper to jot reminder notes to myself and get right back to what I was doing.

Our minds are always beehives of activity. Listen to those buzzes from the inner hive but keep your attention on the honey you are making right now.

Yours to Do. **These are major distractions for me. And these are ways I can eliminate them.**

_____

_____

_____

_____

Two of the major distractions I have to deal with are worry and fatigue. Both disturb my concentration and inhibit my productivity. I have learned to listen for the early signs of worry and fatigue and deal with each before it becomes a debilitating problem.

If I wake up in a bad mood, morning after morning, I'm probably worried. It's time for some brisk games of tennis. If my shoulders get tight while I type, I'm tired. It's time for a tour of the garden. If I play those games of tennis, the worry dissolves in physical activity. If I pull some weeds, I go back to the typewriter refreshed and relaxed. By early intervention, I avoid becoming frazzled and exhausted.

Yours to Do. **These are early signs that I'm worried.**

_____

_____

These are early signs that I'm tired.

_____

_____

An early morning game of tennis or a round of garden grooming may seem to be contradictions to my concentration guideline. They aren't. I have learned that play time contributes to work time.

Play time doesn't just balance work time. Recreation actually enhances concentration. When we ignore our need for time off concentration falters, productivity wanes, energy sags.

Each of us has ways to take time out. What are yours?

***Yours to Do.* These are some good ways for me to take time out.**

_____

_____

_____

We all need organization in our office or work space. But there is such a thing as too much organization! I want office organization that works for me. I don't want to be a slave to it.

I don't like the impersonal look of steel desks. So I don't have one. I hate hunting around in drawers for pencils or pens, so I keep my supplies in baskets. In fact my whole office organization is based on baskets. I have five of them.

My In Basket
My Out Basket
My Pending Basket
My Supply Basket
My Waste Basket

This five-basket system gives me a flow of work that is both informal and smooth. It is also an important time management tool. Here's how it works.

To the right of my work area I have a woven basket for supplies. It's squarish and three inches high. It contains: stamps, postcards, pencil sharpener, Scotch tape, letter opener, liquid paper. Next to it is a frosting can (washed out) full of pens and pencils, a dictionary, and a thesaurus. Whenever I want something in the way of supplies I reach for the Supply Basket. During a busy day things get scattered. But each night I return them to the Supply Basket.

To my left, on my desk, is my In Basket. The In Basket holds any item I plan to deal with soon. (Soon, for me, is today or tomorrow.) This afternoon I find: a letter to answer, a memo to give names of two sales prospects to Kris, an insurance blurb to review, four reminders of incoming phone calls to watch for tomorrow, and two reminders of phone calls to make this evening. All represent items of my business or personal life that are important to process promptly.

On the shelf behind me is my Pending Basket. I think of the Pending Basket as a short-term storage facility. It contains five file folders.

—Banking
—Bills
—Communications going out
—Communications coming in
—Alice (my bookkeeper)

As payment checks come in, I put them in the *Banking* folder. Bills go into the *Bills* folder. Letters or phone calls that I don't need to answer right away go in *Communications going out.* Copies of correspondence that requires answers from the recipient go into *Communications coming in. Alice* is my bookkeeper. Her folder accumulates federal and state tax deposit forms and other accounting odds and ends.

Since I review these folders periodically—banking and communications weekly, bills and Alice monthly—I don't worry about this work never getting done. I've just decided not to do it right now.

Just inside the sliding glass door is my fourth basket, my Out Basket. Into it I put anything that is going somewhere else. Today I find: Two books to return to the library, two copies of *Invest in Yourself* to deliver to a local bookstore, and one postcard to mail. Whenever I go out I check the Out Basket. Sometimes I simply take it along with me.

The fifth basket is my favorite. It's my Waste Basket. Since I leave nothing to memory, but instead write myself notes about everything I want to do, a Waste Basket filled with scrunched pieces of paper represents lots of finished work.

My five baskets help me to manage my time by giving me a place to put any item of business that passes through this office. It forces me to set priorities by deciding whether this item will go into my In Basket or my Pending Basket. It also compels me to record everything on paper.

***Yours to Do.* I have reviewed my office management. I find that it's working pretty well. It will work better if I make these changes.** ____

_____

_____

_____

_____

When I first began writing everything down I felt it was an infuriating waste of time. It turned out to be the best new habit I'd learned in a long time. Here's why.

Every business is deluged with bits of information. People to call. Production schedules to meet. Parts to order. Products to deliver. Your brain deals with this information two ways. It stores it. That is, puts it into memory. It also processes it by relating it to other information.

Don't use your mind as a memory bank. You waste a lot of time trying to remember a phone number, a part's number, a shop's address. A simpler solution is to write it down. Let scraps of paper be your memory.

The second function is by far the more important. Relating one piece of information to another helps you create new ideas, solve problems, and plan the future.

I use notes for just about everything now. Fix the side gate. Call Maryann. Clean out file cabinets. Order symphony tickets by June 1. Clip computer article from business section. As I think of something I write a note, date it, and put it into my In Basket. I find this works especially well for business ideas that pop to mind at inconvenient times—on weekends or as I watch TV. I don't have to waste time or energy trying to remember the idea. I write it down and know where to find it.

***Yours to Do.* Do I waste a lot of time trying to remember things? __**

If I do, how can I solve this time-wasting problem? _____

My last guideline to managing my time is to devote my time to the most important work. And let others do the less important.

Right now the most important work I can do for Upstream Press is to write. I used to drive to Santa Rosa to United Parcel Service to ship books— about an hour round trip. I don't any more. It was a waste of my time. I now ship books through a local shipping service, Post Haste. It's only five minutes away and Nel, the owner, is great at making sure all books get to their destinations.

Take time to figure out your main contribution to your business. If you're a super saleswoman, don't spend your precious time keeping books. Hand it off. If your handmade clothing is exquisite, spend your time producing it. Hand off sales to someone else.

***Yours to Do.* This is my most important contribution to my business.**

These are other things I do that pull me away from this most important work. I'll check the ones I want to hand off to someone else.

12
Money

Money. It's a simple five-letter word, but what power it has. We starve or splurge depending on its availability. We worry about not having it, yet hesitate to have it in abundance.

My son John suggested the ultimate solution—eliminate it. But when he constructed his dream culture free of money he soon discovered that something else would take its place—cowrie shells, elephant tusks, or red beans. Unexpectedly, he had stumbled on an important new understanding of money—it's not magic, it's only a useful tool.

Let's take a look at three ways to judge how well you're using money in your business. The first two—a balance sheet and an income statement—are standard accounting procedures, usually prepared by a professional, to analyze any type of business. The third—a break-even chart—shows the relationship between fixed expenses, variable expenses, and profit.

Each may seem confusing at first. Stick with it. These are important concepts to understand. Let's start with the more familiar of the two.

A Schedule C "Profit or Loss from a Business or Profession" prepared for the federal government at tax time is an income statement. For those of you who haven't seen one yet, it looks pretty much like the one in the "Yours to Do" section that follows.

With one embellishment, that form can become an analytic tool of great value. Here's how. Convert all expense figures to a percentage of sales. By doing so, you create easily understandable relationships between what's coming into your business and what's going out.

Yours to Do. Start from scratch or use your Schedule Cs from the past two years to fill in the income statement. After you have entered all the figures, divide each expense category by the sales income to obtain a percentage of sales. For instance, if you show sales income of $41,000 and telephone expenses of $830, then telephone expenses represent 2% of the money you brought in through sales.

How do the percentages look? Sometimes you can spot an immediate hole to plug. Utility costs high? Remember to turn the lights off when you leave. Big telephone bills? Think before you call long distance; maybe a letter will do just as well. Office supply costs high? Consider recycling

INCOME STATEMENT

	FIRST YEAR		SECOND YEAR	
SALES INCOME	$	100%	$	100%
COST OF GOODS				
GROSS PROFIT				
OPERATING EXPENSES				
RENT				
WAGES				
UTILITIES				
TELEPHONE				
INSURANCE				
ACCT / LEGAL				
TRAVEL				
OFFICE SUPPLIES				
ADVERTISING				
REPAIR / MAINTENANCE				
TAXES / LICENSES				
CAR EXPENSE				
BAD DEBTS				
OTHER				
TOTAL OPERATING				
NET PROFIT				

your wastepaper. A high percentage of bad debts? Tighten up your collection of receivables. Any percent of decrease you achieve in expenses will directly increase your percentage of net profit. That's a great incentive to watch these percentages carefully.

How are the percentages holding from year one to year two? Is your cost of goods, as percentages of sales, the same this year as last year? If not, why? Have your supply costs increased while your price to customers remained the same? Or is there another hole? The owner of a natural food store discovered employee pilferage when she looked into a cost-of-goods percentage that seemed abnormally high.

How's the bottom-line percentage of profit? Is it growing or holding steady from year to year? Is it dropping? This is the real acid test that tells you if bigger is really better. Remember, 100% increase in sales may double the work but may not double the profit.

If you own a retail business, compare your percentages to figures for similar businesses. Use a handy booklet published by National Cash Register called "Expenses in Retail Business." Available from local NCR offices for a $1.50 charge, it lists percentages based on sales, such as you've prepared here, for different types of retail operations—beauty salons and fast food restaurants, for example.

* * *

Now that you have a better understanding of an income statement, let's work up a balance sheet for your business. A balance sheet is like a snapshot. It shows a picture of your business at one specific point in time. It's called a balance sheet because it shows, on one side of the scale, what the business owns. That amount is always balanced by business debts plus the owner's share that appears on the other side of the scale.

Anything a business owns is considered an asset. Cash in the bank. Inventory. Deposits made to phone or utility companies. Bills that have been prepaid. Money customers owe you, called accounts receivable. These receivables are usually entered on the balance sheet with an allowance for bad debt—money you won't be able to collect if someone skips town.

Other assets are equipment or tools used in the business. Larger items such as major pieces of equipment show on the balance sheet with an adjustment for accumulated wear and tear—called depreciation. In other words, equipment is less valuable now than the day you bought it.

***Yours to Do.* Make today's date your balance sheet date. List all assets as they are today—today's bank balance, today's amount of receivables, today's inventory levels. It will take a bit of work to find this information but it's worth it.**

If you have no assets in a particular category, put *none.* Don't forget to subtract the figures in parentheses.

ASSETS

Cash in bank .... _____

Receivables .... _____

    Allowance for bad debt .... (_____)

Inventory.. _____

Prepaid bills.. _____

Equipment and tools................................... _____

    Accumulated depreciation .... (_____)

Other .... _____

                                        Total assets   _____

Now let's look at the other side of the balance sheet. Any amount your business owes is a liability. Bills from suppliers are accounts payable—a liability. Loans from bankers or friends are notes payable—a liability. Payroll taxes not yet handed over to Uncle Sam—a liability. Sales taxes collected from customers but not yet mailed to the agency in charge—a liability.

Yours to Do. **List your liabilities. Use the same date you did for the asset side of the balance sheet.**

LIABILITIES

Accounts payable .... _____

Notes payable .... _____

Accrued taxes... _____

Other .... _____

                                    Total liabilities   _____

Now figure out what share of the business you own.

Yours to Do. **Subtract total liabilities from total assets. The figure left over is the owner's share. That figure is also called net worth or owner's equity.**

                     Total assets   _____

                     Total liabilities   _____

                     Owner's equity   _____

It is possible to come up with a negative figure in owner's equity. Like a fever of 105°, a negative figure for owner's equity is a symptom of serious illness. Seek professional help immediately!

To complete the balance sheet add owner's equity to the list of liabilities. It is, in theory, money that your business owes you. It is the variable that creates the balance for which a balance sheet is famous.

Yours to Do. **Summarize your assets and liabilities in the balance sheet. Total assets and total liabilities *must* be the same figure.**

BALANCE SHEET

Assets		Liabilities	
Cash in bank	_____	Accounts payable	_____
Receivables	_____	Notes payable	_____
Allowance for bad debts	(_____)	Accrued taxes	_____
Inventory	_____		
Prepaid bills	_____	Owner's equity	_____
Equipment/tools	_____		
Accumulated depreciation	(_____)		
Total assets	_____	Total liabilities	_____

So now that you've pulled your hair preparing a balance sheet, what can it be used for? Bank credit, for one thing. A banker will determine from your balance sheet a Current Asset Ratio. That is the relationship between the amount you can turn into cash in the next twelve months and the amount you will have to pay off during the same period. A bank officer is looking for a 2:1 ratio—current assets twice as large as current liabilities.

Yours to Do. **Find your Current Asset Ratio by dividing your current assets by your current liabilities.**

My Current Asset Ratio is _____ .

It's almost impossible to go back in time to prepare a balance sheet for last year. Now that you know the procedure, prepare one annually. If you have an accountant ask him or her to prepare one for you each year at tax time.

An annual balance sheet shows the general condition of your business as of a specific date. An annual income statement shows how you got into that condition, as well as pinpointing important details about income and expenses. The third chart gives you a way to graph the relationships between different expenses and profit. It's called a break-even chart.

In order to create a break-even chart you need three pieces of information.

1. The monthly sales revenue you want twelve months hence.
2. The total of fixed expenses each month.
3. The total of variable expenses you will spend monthly when you reach your sales goal.

Each will be graphed on the break-even chart.

Let's start with your sales goal a year from now. If you have a sales projection, use it. If not, you can make a quick estimate, but remember, the readings on this chart are only as good as the information you put into them.

Yours to Do. **This is my current monthly sales level.** _____

This is my sales goal twelve months from now. _____

Now to expenses. There are two kinds of expenses in any business—fixed expenses and variable expenses. If you have a retail shop you pay rent on the place if five customers come in or fifty. Rent is a fixed expense. The amount you pay does not depend on your sales income.

Other expenses are variable. They do depend on income from sales. For example, at the Treillage Shop, I ordered wallpaper from a supplier *only* when a customer ordered it from me. I did not keep any in inventory. For me, wallpaper was a variable expense. It increased or decreased with the number of sales I made.

Yours to Do. **On the facing page is a list of business expenses. Which are fixed expenses and which expenses depend on your sales level? Mark F for a fixed expense and record the monthly amount you pay. You don't expect these figures to change over the next twelve months. Mark the variable expenses with a V. These expenses will rise as your sales rise. Enter the monthly amount you expect to be paying in each category when you reach your sales goal. Total each column.**

On page 42 is a sample break-even chart. It shows monthly sales levels across the bottom and monthly expenses along the side. The business shown has fixed monthly expenses of $800 (charted with a straight

	F / V	FIXED EXPENSES AMT. PAID MONTHLY	VARIABLE EXPENSES AMT. ANTICIPATED WITH SALES GOAL
INVENTORY			
WAGES			
SALARIES			
EQUIPMENT			
MAINTENANCE			
RENT			
UTILITIES			
INSURANCE			
ACCOUNTING / LEGAL			
TRAVEL			
SUPPLIES			
ADVERTISING			
TAXES			
CAR EXPENSE			
SHIPPING			
OTHER			
TOTAL			

line), sales goal of $5,000 monthly (charted as —·—) and estimated vari-
able monthly expenses of $3,000 (charted as — — —). The break-even
point occurs at $1,750 in sales a month. That sales amount will cover both
fixed and variable costs.

More important, the chart shows the relationship between profits and
variable costs and how each grows with sales. It's a relationship most small
businesses ignore!

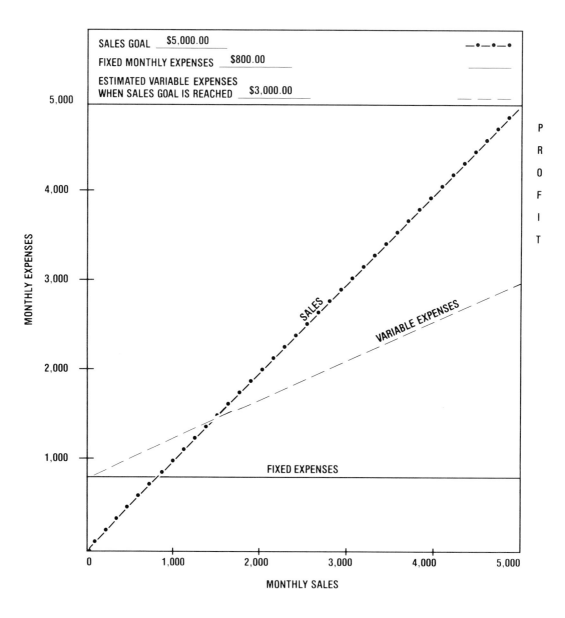

Yours to Do. **Here is a blank break-even chart. Enter your sales goal, fixed monthly expenses, and estimated variable expenses at the top. Chart your fixed expenses across the bottom with a straight line. Chart your sales goal on a diagonal —·—. Begin with 0 in the lower left corner. Chart your variable expenses with — — —. Begin the line for your variable expenses in the lower left of the chart but *on top of your fixed expenses.***

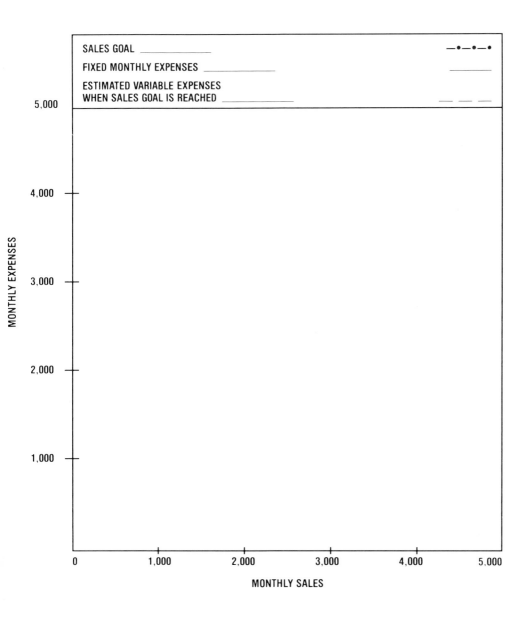

SALES GOAL _____   —·—·—•

FIXED MONTHLY EXPENSES _____   _____

ESTIMATED VARIABLE EXPENSES
WHEN SALES GOAL IS REACHED _____   — — —

MONTHLY EXPENSES

5,000

4,000

3,000

2,000

1,000

0   1,000   2,000   3,000   4,000   5,000

MONTHLY SALES

PART THREE

THE BUSINESS SIDE OF BUSINESS

In the first two parts of *Running Your Business Successfully* you took a look at your business as a big picture. Now it's time to concentrate on details. Both views are equally important.

I have three rules I apply to the details of my business. Make a poster of these rules. Tack it on your office wall where you will see it every day. Learn them by heart. And apply them to every aspect of your business from choice of advertising media to suppliers.

Rule 1   Consider each new business move a test.
Rule 2   Watch for results—not what you expect to happen but what actually does happen.
Rule 3   Cut your losses. This rule applies to both money and people.

RULE 1   CONSIDER EACH NEW BUSINESS MOVE A TEST

Rule 1 reminds me to temper my enthusiasm with healthy skepticism. I consider each new business move as a test. ONLY A TEST. A new advertising campaign may produce sales—but it may not. A new accountant and attorney may solve the problem of slow information exchange—but they may not be any better than the last two. A new supplier may promise faster service—but may not deliver.

Rule 1 also encourages me to move slowly and carefully. A new advertising campaign could involve $10,000 to revamp logo, store sign, newspaper layout, brochure, and business cards or $1,000 for a part of the package. I'd choose to spend $1,000—as a test. A new supplier could drop-ship all the drapery lining I need for the next three months. I'd order two bolts instead—as a test. My new accountant seems jolly and competent. I'll ask for a small piece of work to be returned to me in two weeks—as a test.

RULE 2   WATCH FOR RESULTS

Rule 2 cautions me to watch for results. Projections are fine. Expectations are dandy. Promises are nice. I don't count on any of them. I watch for results. The advertising agent projects a sales increase with a new brochure. Great! I know my sales level now. I'll watch with interest the new sales results. My fabric supplier promises me delivery in three days. Wonderful! I'll check the bolts into inventory the day they arrive.

Rule 2 also warns me that my expectations can sometimes override my practical good sense. I may so badly want the new advertising campaign to produce sales, in order to finance a long-awaited ski vacation, that I ignore the actual outcome. My fabric supplier has so blinded me with her charm and wit that I don't realize a week has passed and my lining fabric is still undelivered.

RULE 3   CUT YOUR LOSSES

Rule 3 gently reminds me that I owe my first loyalty to myself and the business I've created. Survival for us may sometimes mean disappointment or disillusionment for other people.

Dismissing an accountant with whom I've worked for over ten years is not easy. But if he is no longer giving the prompt service my business needs, it's necessary. Telling a charming supplier, who's a marvelous lunch companion, that I'll no longer order from her because of delivery problems is distressing but necessary. Breaking up a partnership that is no longer working smoothly can be devastating but necessary. I've found that cutting business losses always seems to involve cutting people. If it were simply a matter of money it would be much easier.

Rule 3 helps me to understand that I come first. My personal vision of my business is very dear to me. The livelihood I draw from it is both necessary and important. I can't afford to let others destroy either.

While you are doing the following chapters, consider each subpart of your business as a test. Record the results of your early business decisions. Find the losses—in both money and people—that you need to cut. Learn to run your business with this general principle: if it works, keep it; if it doesn't work, chuck it.

13
Does My Business Name
Still Fit My Business?

Frequently a business name is a lucky charm. You may have chosen it because a certain name appealed to your sense of fun or your optimism for the future. I don't like tampering with lucky charms but sometimes it's necessary to make adjustments.

For example, the original name of my first business was Treillage Interiors. I worked out of my home with that business name for six months. Later I opened a small retail shop in the downtown business district. The original name seemed too sophisticated for the new surroundings to I changed it to the Treillage Shop. I retained my talisman but refined it and slightly changed the image.

Choosing a new type style or creating a new logo are other ways to fine-tune business names. Upstream Press went through such changes. Our original logo looked like this:

We found the format awkward on a letterhead so we changed it to this:

UPSTREAM PRESS

While retaining bold, simple characters we eliminated the clumsy box appearance.

Sometimes a business outgrows its name. A giftware manufacturer starts with a single product—decorative glass boxes. Then she adds two others items—plastic note holders and stained glass Christmas ornaments. The original name, Bonny Boxes, no longer fits the business.

One solution is to change Bonny Boxes from the business name to a line name, choose another line name for the stained glass ornaments, and put both under a new business name that is more descriptive and inclusive—Bonny Gifts, for example.

Beware of drastic name changes! Make small changes that tell your customer more clearly who you are and what you do. Retain large elements of your previous name. This gives your customers a feeling of continuity and stability. Change your image gradually. If you are not careful during this process you may lose customers.

Yours to Do. **This is my business name.** _____

This is how customers react to my business name. _____

_____

Do I like the way they react? _____

If not, what reaction do I want? _____

_____

These are small changes I can make in my business name that will help me tell customers more clearly who I am and what I do—and

get the reaction I want. _____

_____

_____

These are possible new names for my business. In each case I've been careful not to change too much. I have included large elements of my old name in my new one.

_____   _____

_____   _____

_____   _____

14
What Is My Current Mix
of Products and Services?

There are four major types of businesses—manufacturing, wholesaling, retailing, and service. Very few businesses fall exclusively into one category. Most businesses are a mix of two or more.

As the business grows the mix may change. An aerobics studio, originally conceived as strictly a service business, begins to sell exercise togs and natural cosmetics. It now mixes retail and service operations. A manufacturer of water sports equipment now leads recreational tours to demonstrate and promote her equipment. Part of her business is manufacturing. She has also added a service element. A retailer of women's intimate apparel has designed a lacy chemise. She is now manufacturing the design for her customers as well as wholesaling dozens to other shops. Her business has become a combination of retail, wholesale, and manufacturing.

Yours to Do. **When I started, my business was a combination of these elements. These were the percentages of income each element contributed.**

Original Mix	Original Percentage of Business Income
Manufacturing	_____
Wholesaling	_____
Retailing	_____
Service	_____

This is how it looks today.

Today's Mix	Today's Percentage of Business Income
Manufacturing	_____
Wholesaling	_____
Retailing	_____
Service	_____

Study these trends in your business. Are you heading in the right direction or being sidetracked?

For those of you looking for new areas of expansion, be aware of the possibilities of branching into another type of business. Add the element of retailing to your service business. Or service to your retail business.

Yours to Do. Here are some bright ideas about how to add another type of business to my current operation.

_____

_____

_____

_____

_____

15

What Are My Best Profit Centers?

Think of your business as a giant chocolate chip cookie. The whole cookie is your business. Each chocolate chip is a profit center. Good chocolate chip cookies are loaded with chips. Growing businesses are loaded with profit centers. A profit center is a single item, a group of items, a single service, or a category of services that produce a profit for you.

In a suburban bookstore, science fiction novels may be one profit center and gothic novels another. Other profit centers include calendars, textbooks, bookmarks, magazines, nonfiction, and self-help books. In a college town, textbooks might be the best profit center and gothic novels the poorest.

For a mushroom farmer, wholesale sales are one profit center, retail sales another. Each category of sales is a separate profit center. Teaching gourmet cooking classes at the mushroom ranch is a third. Recently she added a fourth—selling compost.

The owner of a shop that provides services to small business people acts as an answering service, a shipper of parcels, a receiver of mail, a bookkeeper, a copy maker. Her business has five profit centers.

Upstream Press currently has two product profit centers—*Invest in Yourself* and this book. It also has two service profit centers—the classes I teach at local community colleges and the consulting work I do with other women business owners.

Analyze your business. Find your profit centers. Don't be fooled by some part of your business that *seems* to be producing. Make sure that it is producing.

Use four criteria to analyze your profit centers—the time you put into that area of your business, the money you put into it, the physical space you give it (especially important for retailers), and the profit you get out. Develop a record-keeping system that helps you track each profit center. Use the chart on page 55 to study your profit centers.

Yours to Do. Use the Profit Centers chart to study your profit centers for the past quarter. Assign the correct proportion of gross sales to each profit center. Enter the cost of goods for each profit center and calculate your dollar profit. Then calculate the percentage of profit from each center. Study the space used for each profit center and assign a percentage. Calculate the percentage of time you spend on

each profit center. Note any hassles you can attribute to any specific profit center.

Here are some examples of discoveries you might make after your study. The collegiate bookstore owner finds no surprises in her top profit center—textbooks. The gross sales are good, cost of sales as expected, profits in line with sales. Time and floor space devoted to this profit center are in proportion to sales.

She does find a surprise in her magazine profit center, however. Only a few magazines sell really well, the rest are dogs. She spends an unreasonable amount of time straightening shelves, bundling returns at the end of the month, and watching for thefts. Though magazines produce only 2% of the monthly gross sales, they take up 10% of the floor space. She's thinking of dropping magazines altogether.

The mushroom farmer had the idea six months ago to advertise spent medium as compost and mulch. She realizes now what a very good idea it was. Instead of her paying a commercial hauler to cart the stuff away, local gardeners are buying it eagerly. She is now selling 50% of the waste product. It's accounting for 5% of her gross sales monthly and she's saving the price of the hauler. With a little additional advertising she figures she can sell all the spent medium and save the entire disposal cost, thereby upping her profit in two ways.

Yours to Do. **After studying my profit centers, I find no surprises in these areas.**

_____

_____

_____

_____

I did find some surprises in these areas.

_____

_____

_____

These are changes I want to make because of my findings.

_____

_____

_____

PROFIT CENTERS

NAME OF PROFIT CENTER	GROSS SALES	COST OF GOODS (incl. labor)	PROFIT	% PROFIT	% TIME USED	% SPACE USED
1	$	$	$	%	%	%
2						
3						
4						
5						
6						
7						
8						
TOTALS	$	$	$	100%	100%	100%

16
Who Are My Customers?

Learning about your customer is an ongoing process. The customer you originally planned to attract may not be the customer you're actually attracting.

I planned the Treillage Shop to attract the young families moving into the new subdivisions on the east side of town. I located the shop, however, in the downtown shopping center, which was on the west side of town. The Petaluma River seems to present an invisible barrier. East side residents don't shop on the west side of town, or vice versa. I soon realized that my best and most frequent customers were the older established families on the west side. Luckily, my shop was as attractive to them as to the customers I originally wanted to serve.

Some parts of the shop did change as the tastes of the clientele became more apparent. I dropped a line of quilted, washable cotton bedspreads and window displays featuring children's rooms. My clients had already raised their children. Washability in bedspreads is no advantage to women who no longer worry about spilled milk.

I also found that one of the newest fabric ideas—patchwork quilt designs—had little appeal to my clients. Raised in the Depression, they associated patches with poverty!

It's important to remain curious about your customers. Gather as much information about them as possible. Friendly questions about their families, club affiliations, or recreational activities give you a better understanding of who they are, what they like, and how they live.

Wholesalers and manufacturers are in the awkward position of having intermediaries between themselves and their ultimate customers. It's important to remain in contact with your end-users. If you're a manufacturer of toy products for five-year-olds, keep in contact with that age group and their parents. Your original product testers (daughter and friends) may be more interested in boys than bunnies by now.

Yours to Do. **This is a description of the customer I *thought* I'd be serving. I made the sketch before I opened my business. It includes information on my customer's age, sex, income level, housing style, and family life. It also includes other information about him or her**

that was important for me at that time. _____

_____

_____

_____

_____

After being in business for _____ **months/years these are changes or additions I need to make in that customer description.**

_____

_____

_____

_____

As a wholesaler or manufacturer I need to keep in touch with the end-user of my products. These are ways I can do it. _____

_____

_____

17

Can My Location Function Better?

Many women are choosing their homes as their places of business. I know wholesalers, retailers, manufacturers, and service businesses—all women-owned and all home-based. For a lot of us, it is a sensible choice, both personally and financially.

Home offices can be improved—just like other aspects of your business. Now is the time for a review. Have you outgrown the dining-room table as your activity center? Can you improve your efficiency with new telephone services such as call forwarding, call waiting, or a less expensive long distance service? Is it time to graduate from boxes to file cabinets for record storage? Is it time just to clean up and throw out?

Yours to Do. **These are ways to improve my home office.**

_____

_____

_____

_____

Home offices are not the only locations that could use a thorough spring cleaning. If you've been doing business in a shop, loft, or manufacturing plant for more than six months, you've accumulated a lot of junk. Gather it up and toss it out.

Also, check on maintenance problems—burned-out lights, loose carpet, sticky locks. Junk and poor maintenance distract your energy. Plan a time for cleanup and repair. It's part of business to keep your location in good working order.

Yours to Do. **These are maintenance problems that I need to take care of. This is when I will do them.**

_____

_____

_____

Are you a retail shop owner? Set aside time to reassess your use of floor space and display areas. Are they in line with the percentages of profit they produce? Would it be better to move the quilted potholders closer to your cookware store cash register to encourage purchase as impulse items? Would pots and pans be better displayed hanging than sitting on shelves?

Lively, creative displays encourage people to come in—if just to browse. They'll be back to buy later. Learn new display ideas from trade magazines and from your competitors. Borrow the best for your store.

After you have completed this initial review, set aside time, at least every three months, to look again. A lot of small shop owners neglect such periodic reviews. Suddenly they find themselves doing business with dirty windows and dingy displays.

Yours to Do. I have completed my review of floor space and display areas. These are the changes I want to make.

_____

_____

_____

I want to do a similar review in _____ months. I'll enter the date now in my planning calendar.

18

Is My Competition Changing?

Keeping track of competition involves studying both the big picture and its details. The big picture points out business trends that affect your business. The details highlight individual competitors.

You can research national trends in magazines such as *Business Week* or newspapers such as *The Wall Street Journal.* Don't be intimidated by such impressive names. Just get trial subscriptions and test them. Use magazines and newspapers to gather information that will help your business survive and thrive. Even the smallest business owner in the smallest town is part of national trends. Each business is either going with a trend, going against it, or starting a new one. You need to know where your business stands.

Upstream Press is riding the crest of a major national trend—women's growing interest in self-employment. In 1977 women owned 702,000 businesses in this country. That represented 7.1% of all businesses. In 1983 women owned 3,700,000 businesses or 25% of all businesses.

I knew two years ago that I was working with a trend. But it's nice to have its importance verified by the New York *Times.*

Other sources of information about trends and competition are trade magazines. Do you subscribe to one or more? If not, go to the library, find *Writer's Market,* open to the listing of "Trade, Technical and Professional Journals," jot down appropriate names and addresses, and order your subscriptions today. Don't deny yourself these valuable sources of information.

Yours to Do. **These are the ways I keep in touch with national trends affecting my type of business.** _____

_____

This is how my business fits into those trends. _____

_____

_____

_____

_____

_____

Gathering information about business trends is the first step in studying the competition. Next, examine individual competitors.

When you opened your business you were convinced that your product or service had two strong qualities. It was different. It was better. Business situations change rapidly, however. Do you have any new competitor whose product or service resembles yours? If so, it's time for another look. Find ways to redefine how your product is *still* different and *still* better.

When I opened the Treillage Shop it was the only decorating shop in town. Within two years I had three competitors. Each of us sold window covering, wallpaper, and carpet. But was my shop really like the others? Of course not.

But after losing the special status of "the only decorating shop in Petaluma" I had to find new ways to explain to my customers how the Treillage Shop was *still* different and *still* better.

I decided to emphasize our drapery manufacturing operation. Since we manufactured custom drapes right in the shop, we were different from our competitors. Since I took the time and effort to supervise the operation myself our quality control was better. My constant message became, "We manufacture right here so we can guarantee you better quality."

Yours to Do. Here's a list of the new competitors that have appeared since I opened my business.

_____

_____

_____

Here are two ways that my business is *still* different from and *still* better than any of the competitors.

_____

_____

_____

Here is a simple way to explain to my customers how my business is different and how it is better.

_____

_____

_____

19

Are My Suppliers Performing Well?

When a supplier makes a delivery commitment, expect her to keep it. Plain and simple. You run your business smoothly and efficiently. Don't waste valuable time and energy dealing with excuses. Or hold up production schedules because of supply problems.

Make your first criterion for judging a supplier consistent on-time delivery.

A second criterion is fair, competitive pricing. Don't be penalized too much for buying in low volume, though understand that certain price adjustments are necessary for less than huge orders.

Also expect consistent quality in the goods or services you purchase. Insist on a low flaw rate. It's a term that applies equally well to the amount of usable yards on a bolt of drapery fabric or the amount of usable advice in an hour with your accountant.

Rate your suppliers also on their ability to produce understandable, trouble-free billing. Verifying obscure codes or unspecified charges absorbs your time. Settling account errors, if they occur, is not only time-consuming but frustrating.

A good sales representative can be an invaluable liaison between your business and the supplier she represents. Use your reps to assist you in any problem areas that may arise. If they don't provide a solution promptly, it's an indication of a poor supplier.

Let your suppliers know you expect 100% perfect performance from them. Of course you won't get it. But it's better to expect 100% and get 85% than to expect 75% and get 50%. Thank-you notes to those sales reps or suppliers who are performing well show your appreciation. They also cement the good working relationship you've already established.

As a new business, you may have settled for suppliers who were willing to do business with you. But as a business grows and purchase volume rises, you gain both status and negotiating clout. Use them!

***Yours to Do.* Use the Suppliers Chart to rate your suppliers. Put a check mark for any category in which that supplier is giving less than satisfactory performance. Do you need to start looking for some alternative suppliers?**

SUPPLIERS CHART

	ON-TIME DELIVERY	COMPETITIVE PRICING	LOW FLAW RATE	TROUBLE-FREE BILLING	PROMPT ATTENTION TO PROBLEMS	GOOD SALES REP	COMMENTS
1							
2							
3							
4							
5							
6							
7							
8							
9							
10							

20
Is It Time to Change My Prices?

When you opened your business you set a price on your product or service. Was it the right price when you opened? Is it the right price now? Or is it time to make some adjustments to your price structure?

I stated three laws of pricing in *Invest in Yourself*. They are important enough to restate here.

Law 1. The right selling price includes all costs.
Law 2. The right selling price includes a reasonable profit.
Law 3. The right selling price is a price your customer will pay.

Let's see what happens to profits and prices in three different businesses after they've been open for a year or so.

An herb farmer started two years ago to package herb seeds for sale. Since then she has branched into selling small starter plants in six-packs. Having tracked her costs carefully and having passed all obvious increases on to her customers, she feels as though she has followed the First Law of Pricing.

In most ways she has. Last season, wholesale seed prices increased—she raised her retail prices to include these new costs. The price of plastic six-packs went up—she adjusted her retail prices to include those new costs. She hired helpers to transplant—and passed on employee costs to her customers.

Are there any other increases in costs that have slipped by? On closer examination she finds two—labor burden expenses for her three employees and utility costs for her well pump.

Her accountant recently pointed out that, along with the wages she pays, she is also contributing an additional 12% just to have those employees on her payroll. Though she is paying her employees $300 a week, they are costing her $336 a week. The additional expense of $36 is labor burden. It includes her contribution to FICA and the cost of state disability insurance and workers' compensation insurance.

While reading the local newspaper, the herb farmer notices a story announcing another public utility rate increase. Her well pump will cost even more to run this year than last year.

In setting this season's prices she needs to take both costs into consideration, so that her new selling price will include all costs.

Yours to Do. **I last reviewed my prices on _____ (date).**

64

Since then I have had these increases in my cost of goods.

_____

_____

_____

_____

Did I pass these new costs on to my customers? _____

My labor costs have risen this much. _____

Did I pass these new costs on to my customers? _____

I have had these increases in my operating expenses.

_____

_____

_____

_____

Have I made adjustments in my selling price to cover these increases in operating costs? _____

These are the price adjustments I need to make so that the selling price of my product or service covers all my costs. _____

_____

_____

_____

The Second Law of Pricing states that the right selling price includes a reasonable profit. Two women, partners in a toy manufacturing business, recently made price adjustments to conform to this law. Here's their situation.

They introduced a toy product three years ago. After computing all costs of goods and manufacturing labor costs, they added 75% as a markup* to arrive at their price to wholesalers. They used a 75% markup even though they knew that 100% was standard. Since they were using

---

*For those of you who are not clear on the difference between markup and margin, here's another explanation. It took me six months and five explanations to get it straight.

Markup is a term used to describe a percentage of profit. It is the difference between the purchase price and the selling price stated as a percentage of the *purchase price*. If you purchase an item for $50 and sell it for $100, your markup is 100%. If you purchase an item for $50 and sell it for $75, your markup is 50%.

Margin is also a term used to describe a percentage of profit. It is the difference between the purchase price and the selling price stated as a percentage of the *selling price*. If you purchase an item for $50 and sell it for $100, your profit margin is 50%. If you purchase an item for $50 and sell it for $75, your profit margin is 33.3%.

their homes as their business location, thus keeping their operating expenses low, they figured they could afford a lesser markup.

Now they are ready to put a second product onto the market. They have decided to use a full 100% markup. Over the last three years they have worked hard in their business. They want to increase their profits to a level more in line with the time and energy they put in. If they want to make a reasonable profit, they will need to get a full 100% markup on each item sold.

Yours to Do. **Using your Income Statement from Part Two, compute your gross and net profits. Enter the figures below.**

Gross sales for last year	$ _____
Cost of goods	− $ _____
Labor costs (if not included in cost of goods)	− $ _____
Gross profit	$ _____

Divide gross profit by gross sales to arrive at a gross profit percentage.

My gross profit as a percentage is _____ %.

Gross profit	$ _____
Operating expenses	− $ _____
Net profit	$ _____

Divide net profit by gross sales to arrive at a net profit percentage.

My net profit margin as a percentage is _____ %.

Am I making a reasonable gross profit? _____

Am I making a reasonable net profit? _____

What adjustments do I need to make to my prices to make a reasonable gross profit? _____

_____

_____

What adjustments do I need to make to my prices to make a reasonable net profit? _____

_____

_____

If you increase the price of your product or service will your customers still be willing to pay your price? Or will you lose your customers?

I struggled with this question based on the Third Law of Pricing at the Treillage Shop. When I opened the shop I did not pass on to my customers shipping charges on wallpaper orders. I was getting a generous 50% discount from suppliers eager to establish themselves in northern California, and UPS shipping charges were minimal.

Over the first two years the situation changed drastically. After establishing themselves, my original suppliers decreased my discount. I took on other lines with similar skimpy profit margins. UPS substantially increased shipping rates.

My wallpaper sales had disintegrated from a good profit item to almost a courtesy sale. I couldn't negotiate any additional discount from my suppliers because of my low purchase volume. I couldn't increase the price of the wallpaper since each pattern was marked with a retail price. The only remaining option to rescue faltering profits was to pass on to my customers UPS shipping charges. But would my customers be willing to pay the additional price or would they walk out, insulted, to shop elsewhere? I feared the worst.

I tested the Third Law of Pricing and found that retail price of wallpaper plus shipping charges was still the right price for wallpaper in my shop. My customers paid the combined charges without comment.

Yours to Do. **Have I been hesitating to change the price of my product or service because I've wondered if my customer would pay my new price?** _____

_____

How can I experiment with the price of my product or service to test the Third Law of Pricing?

_____

_____

_____

Follow the three laws of pricing. Don't undervalue the monetary worth of the products you produce or the services you provide. When you do, you deny yourself the just profit you deserve.

21

Do I Have a Workable
Market Plan?

Creating and sustaining a good marketing effort in a small business is tough. At the same time it's the very core of your business growth. Without a plan, your approach to the marketplace is hit and/or miss.

Yet it's obvious that small businesses can't use the marketing techniques of a giant corporation. We don't have either the financial or the professional resources to introduce a new product the way Detroit introduces a new car model. But what are the alternatives?

In the course of doing business I have found a lot of ways to market my products and services that use only a small portion of the resources available to a giant corporation. And you have too. Here are some more valuable suggestions to enhance your marketing efforts. Make each of them part of your market plan.

Suggestion 1 Make sure your customers can find you.
Suggestion 2 Let your friends generate customers.
Suggestion 3 Create a good mailing list and use it.
Suggestion 4 Become an expert in your field and let your community know it.

Remember that customers are all those interested in your product or service—not just people you have already sold to. Make sure your customers can find you.

If you are a manufacturer of children's clothes, does your label contain sufficient information for a snoopy buyer to track you down? A retail store, of course, may object to your including name, full address, and phone number on your label. It may tempt customers to bypass them and shop from you direct. But a retailer would not object to a label that includes just your business name and city and state. With a listing in your local phonebook, that's sufficient information for an astute baby clothes buyer for a large retail chain to contact you.

Service businesses have to be more inventive about ways to lead customers back to them. If you give therapeutic massages, it's not possible to glue your label on the arm you've just treated. But you could send home a small bottle of massage oil with the customer. Its label identifies you as the source of both the oil and the massage.

A caterer can supply matches for all her parties imprinted with her business and number. A color consultant can pass out a summary of her talk to a women's club typed on her letterhead. In both cases these business owners have found ways that allow new customers to find them—not just next week but next year as well.

Don't rely solely on business cards. They are good but they are only a start. Include as an important part of your market plan fail-safe methods that will help your customers locate you.

***Yours to Do.* These are the current methods I use to help my customers locate me.**

_____

_____

_____

Since it's such an important part of my market plan, I need to make these changes and additions. It will make my system fail-safe.

_____

_____

_____

I find business owners reluctant to use their friends as business promoters. Yet I think it's important to include them in your market plan. If you've lived in a community for five years or more you probably have a wide circle of reasonably good friends—people you know through either social or work activities. Say fifteen or twenty. These friends of yours have friends who in turn have friends.

You have fifteen friends. Each of your friends has fifteen friends. And each of your friends' friends has fifteen friends. Figuring on some back-looping friendships, that is a network of 2,000 to 3,375 people you can reach by talking to fifteen people. Is it reasonable for a business woman to pass up the opportunities for over 2,000 *free* business contacts?

But in order to make your friends effective in finding customers, those fifteen or twenty people have to know what you do. How many times have you asked a friend to help you find a product or service? Do you know a reliable auto mechanic? Where can I find a knockout dress for Helen's wedding? Who can teach me to recane Granny's antique chair? Questions like these always come up in conversations between friends. All you need to do is add clarity and depth to your friends' knowledge of you as a business person. Give them important details to pass down their information channel.

Define yourself. If you are a caterer, explain: "I love to do vegetable pâtés. I create beautiful platters. I'm most effective at a party for twenty or less." Add details about your charges. A wardrobe planner may say, "I will review an entire wardrobe free of charge. But I charge $30 an hour to go shopping with a client." Include information about times available or working environment. A family therapist may say, "I usually meet clients in my home between 8 A.M. and 5 P.M. on weekdays. I do work some evenings but never on Saturdays or Sundays. I have two shaggy dogs and six cats. If a client is allergic to animals we can arrange to meet somewhere else." Add customers' evaluation of your work. A photographer may say, "Some people consider my photos sentimental and romantic. Others consider them sympathetically realistic." Without such clear statements, your friends cannot find customers for you.

One of the simplest ways to interest your friends in your business is to give them some of your product or a demonstration of your service. A physical therapist specializes in hands. She gives a demonstration of massage techniques to her professional friends. She has three referrals the following week. A deli owner is featuring a new line of barbecued almonds. She passes them around at the church picnic. Members come in to buy their own supplies on Monday.

With each such move you give your friends more credible information about your product or service. They will pass it on to their friends and generate dozens of new customers for you. But that's not the only thing that happens. You also deepen your relationships by taking the time and making the effort to share yourself and your important area of expertise with your friends.

***Yours to Do.* How do I feel about including my friends in my market plan?**

_____

_____

_____

Is that a sensible reaction? Why? _____

_____

_____

Here are the names of fifteen or twenty friends with whom I will share information about my business. Some are social friends. Some are business friends.

_____   _____

_____   _____

_____   _____

_____   _____

_____   _____

_____   _____

_____   _____

_____   _____

_____   _____

Here is a clear definition of my business. It includes necessary information on charges, times available, working environment, and reactions of other customers. I will tell my friends this information in person so they can read the excitement and enthusiasm in my eyes. No brochures for my friends!

_____

_____

_____

_____

_____

What samples of my product can I give to my friends?

_____

_____

How can I demonstrate my service to my friends?

_____

_____

_____

_____

_____

Your inventory of fifteen or twenty friends is a beginning of another marketing step—a good mailing list. Add to that list supporters, suppliers, and customers.

People you meet at a cocktail party or weekend religious retreat are candidates for your list if they express interest in what you do. Remember, it's the casual encounter with a supporter six months or a year ago that produces business today.

Suppliers and their sales reps are good additions to your list. Don't underestimate their value in producing new business for you.

Current customers are the last and probably the largest element of your mailing list. You'll need good records to have access to their names, addresses, and phone numbers.

Make it a habit to fill out all sales slips or invoices *completely* so you have the information you need. Equally important is an accurate description of what you sold. Make it detailed enough to remember the item or service easily. If you sold your customer a rocking chair, note the type of wood or the color it was painted. If you gave your customer a massage, note that you worked on the left calf, stiff because of bicycle riding.

As your mailing list grows, so do the security and stability of your business. If someone has been in business for a year and a half and has a mailing list of 120 it's extremely easy to generate new business.

With experience, you'll find ways to help people give you their names and addresses. Avoid tactics such as raffles, however. They tend to give the impression that you are a manipulating, impersonal business owner. A simple request for information "so we can stay in touch" is much better.

Yours to Do. **Do my sales slips or invoices give me the information I need for a mailing list?** _____

If they don't, what changes do I need to make? _____

_____

_____

After reviewing my records I find I currently have this many names I can use on a mailing list.

Friends	_____
Supporters	_____
Suppliers	_____
Customers	_____
Total	_____

Now that you have a mailing list, how are you going to use it? You could use it simply to announce an upcoming sale. That's a good use, but here's a better one.

You, your friends, your supporters, your suppliers, and your customers are a group of people with common interests. You've already demonstrated that fact by dealing with each other. You are, in a very real sense, a community.

But what is your particular role in that community? You're their expert, of course. Use your role as expert to keep in touch with your community.

Be a little abstract when you define your expertise. Do you own a natural food store? Your larger concern is a healthy environment. Do you do word processing? Your expertise is recording, storing, and passing on information. Do you run a flower shop? Your concern is aesthetics, as well as botany.

As you broaden the concept of your expert relationship with your community, you'll find hundreds of things you can do for them—and pass on information about them through your mailing list.

Here are four brief sketches of businesswomen who are acting as experts to their communities.

Name: Carol
Business: Word processing
Expertise: Information storage and transferral

Carol sends out word via her mailing list of fifty that she is having a coffee Thursday afternoon for an author whose book she has just completed. They will discuss advantages and disadvantages of word processing versus typewriting a manuscript. All welcome. Please RSVP.

Name: Karen
Business: Refinishing antiques
Expertise: Appreciation and care of fine furniture

Karen has recently tried a new product designed to nourish older woods. She is thrilled with the results she is getting with the product in her workshop and sends out postcards to 100 on her mailing list announcing the product and recommending its use.

Name: Lila
Business: Gourmet deli
Expertise: Appreciation of fine foods

Lila, who usually imports all of her cheeses, has just found a fine locally produced goat cheese. In order to introduce it to her clients she announces, through a flier to 500, a gala open house next Friday evening. Wine will be served along with samples of the local cheese.

Name: Sachiko
Business: Weaving, using Japanese techniques
Expertise: Japanese crafts and culture

Sachiko, an expert weaver, has a friend visiting from Japan. They decide to put on a demonstration of origami—a Japanese paper folding craft they both learned as children. Sachiko sends out seventy-five invitations for Saturday afternoon with requests for affirmative answers by Thursday.

Becoming an adviser to your community—by sharing your special skills or sources of information—is an exciting addition to any market plan. I use a slight variation on the theme by having Sunday brunches. Once a month I hostess a brunch for sixteen or so people I feel would enjoy meeting each other. I introduce Jim, who's written a book, to Mike, who wants to write one. I introduce Sally, who makes fine folksy clothes, to Jean, whose two daughters would enjoy wearing them. In both cases I'm sharing contacts I've developed in my areas of expertise—writing and women's entrepreneurship.

Yours to Do. **This is a description of my business.**

_____

When I broaden the concept of what I do, this is how I describe my area of expertise.

_____

_____

_____

Listed in the chart are twelve ways I can share my special skills and sources of information with my community. I will incorporate one a month into my market plan.

IDEA 1	IDEA 7
IDEA 2	IDEA 8
IDEA 3	IDEA 9
IDEA 4	IDEA 10
IDEA 5	IDEA 11
IDEA 6	IDEA 12

22

Are My Advertising and Promotion Producing Results?

Putting money into advertising often seems like pouring water down a rat hole. Here's an area where you really have to watch for results and cut your losses. Easy advice to give but hard to follow, since the results of advertising are often so hard to judge. Is that one-column-by-four-inch ad you run weekly in the local advertising gazette really effective? Does that three-times-a-day radio spot on your local station produce customers? Sometimes it's hard to tell.

Wherever possible, include a tag that points out the source of the sale. A retail shoestore advertises a 10% trade-in allowance on kids' old tennis shoes. A mom or dad who brings in smelly tennies as trade-ins has responded to that particular ad. A flower shop advertises a free boutonniere with the purchase of prom flowers. A young man who asks for the freebie has seen your ad. A mail-order bookseller adds Dept 210 or Drawer 210 to the order address. That code tags the response to a specific magazine (coded as #2 in the office) and a specific issue. In this case, 10 stands for the month of October.

Immediate responses account for only a part of the work any particular ad does. There are always customers who forget the kids' old tennis shoes but come in anyhow. There are always shoppers who react to your ad now but don't have a need for your product or service until six months from now. In such cases of delayed response, advertisements designed to sell a special item at a special price adopt a wider function—keeping the name of your business before the public.

One way to test the effectiveness of your advertising is to eliminate it completely for a month or so. The owner of a local do-it-yourself frame shop canceled all her advertising contracts in disgust. She was convinced they were not producing adequate results. Sales dropped drastically. One point was proved. Her advertising was working. The next step was to find out which parts worked the best. With some further experimentation, and a close watch on results, she established an ad campaign calculated to produce the best results for every dollar invested.

Another alternative is to hire an advertising agent. An agent can review your current advertising media, suggest new ones, write copy, design ads, and place them.

An agent not only has extensive knowledge about available advertising media, she also knows where a particular type of customer goes for information. She can suggest radio spots during "A.M. drive time" as the best way to reach your customer as she commutes to work or the "Sporting Green" as the best page to advertise your camping equipment.

Standard agency fees include both direct and indirect charges. When an agency places an ad for you it receives a 17% discount from the advertiser. The agency charges you the regular price (the same amount you'd pay if you placed the ad directly) and pockets the difference.

There will also be additional direct charges for production work—development of an advertising style, creation of an effective ad, artwork, paste-up and layout. The range of production fees—$25 to $100 an hour—varies with geography. Sometimes an agency will negotiate the 17% discount and credit part of it against your production bill. As your business grows, the addition of an advertising expert may be valuable.

Some businesses eliminate advertising completely and concentrate on publicity instead. Free stories on radio or television or in newspapers and magazines become the basis of their public exposure. One front-page story or picture can bring in just as much business as ten back-page ads.

Recently a flower shop alerted the city's newspaper about a Secretaries Week Special. A local he-man would be delivering flowers and plants. For an additional charge he would add a spine-tingling Tarzan yell. A press photographer arrived to photograph the first delivery. The large front-page photo and caption, including newsworthy details (name of recipient, name of the shop, charge for the yell), produced a booming week of sales.

If you can't produce an angle like this to promote your business, consider adding another expert to your staff—a publicist. A publicist's skills and contacts can open many media doors for you. Eighty percent of all newspaper stories are planted by publicists and public affairs directors. These professionals search for the newsworthy side of a business—either straight news about the facts, figures, and progress of the business, or a feature story that highlights human interest aspects.

There are several ways to work with a publicist. Perhaps you'll be moving to a new location. Put a publicist on retainer for the next three months to get the word out. Introducing a new product? Hire a publicist to handle just that project. She will present a proposal including cost estimates. If you like her ideas and the figures are realistic, sign a contract for that specific piece of work.

Maybe you want to handle your own publicity but need some expert direction. Pay for a couple of hours' consultation time. When you notice a business is getting especially good press coverage, contact the owner and ask for her publicist's name.

Look for promotional tie-ins with other businesses. A cookware store offers its pots and pans to decorate a bookstore's display window, which showcases new cookbooks. A restaurant announces that this week's floral decorations come from a certain local florist. Five fitness studios jointly sponsor a health fair and ask local sports retailers to join them.

Yours to Do. These are all the different ways I currently advertise.

_____

_____

_____

_____

_____

I have suspicions that these parts of my advertising campaign aren't producing the results I want.

_____

_____

Are there ways I can test them to prove whether or not they are actually producing? How?

_____

_____

_____

These are the names of three local advertising agents. They have been recommended by small business owners I know. I'll call them to arrange an appointment (no charge!). Maybe we can work together on my advertising.

_____

_____

_____

I received the following free publicity for my business over the past year. _____

_____

_____

_____

These are other publicity ideas I want to present to the media. _____

_____

_____

These are publicity tie-ins I could pursue with other businesses.

_____

_____

_____

23
Do My Records Produce the Information I Need?

Any business generates a lot of raw data. Good business records convert all that raw data into usable information. A stack of sales slips is raw data. Compiled into a mailing list, sorted to indicate profit centers, or filed by date, those sales slips become usable information. A basket of invoices is merely data. Entered onto suppliers' accounts-payable cards or totaled for the week, these same invoices produce usable information. A pile of canceled checks is raw data. Recorded on a spread sheet that breaks down expenditures into operating, production, or salary expenses, these checks are transformed into usable information.

Most business owners don't make enough use of the data they generate. Instead of converting data into useful information they leave it in its original unusable form.

Arranging data into useful information begins with asking questions. What kind of information do I want to know about my business? What information would be helpful to expand sales? What information would help me decrease expenses?

A retail shop owner asks herself, "Can I afford to hire sales help? I'm getting so tired by the end of the week."

She sorts her dated sales slips by the day of the week and discovers that Thursdays and Fridays are her busiest selling days and Mondays her least busy. A year's worth of data indicates that sales help is needed on Thursdays and Fridays but not on Mondays. She has answered her question. "Yes, I can afford sales help, but only for two days a week." The solution is drawn from data already available.

A landscape designer asks, "In what neighborhoods did I generate the most business last year?" She buys a map of the surrounding area, reviews her sales records, and uses push pins to mark locations of her clients. The pins show that 45% of her business occurs in one neighborhood and 30% in another. Taking her study one step further, she learns that these two neighborhoods not only produce a lot of sales, they also produce the majority of her appreciative, easy-to-work-with clients. By using available data, she has answered her initial question. She has also discovered her best base of referrals—enthusiastic clients.

A manufacturer cries, "My cash flow is crazy! Sales are up but I never seem to have money in the bank. What's happening?" A review of her financial records shows that information is not available. Owing to her bookkeeper's illness last month, the records are not up to date. No data has been converted to usable information.

QUESTIONS	RAW DATA NEEDED	HOW DO I GATHER IT?	ADDITIONAL INFORMATION I NEED AND HOW TO GATHER IT
1			
2			
3			
4			
5			

Analyze your business records. Review the ways you gather data on the flow of money, things, and people through your business. Then formulate questions you want to have answered. Are your current records producing the needed raw data to get those answers?

***Yours to Do.* These are questions I have about customers, cash flow, inventory, suppliers, discounts, profit levels, and expenses. This is the raw data I need to get those answers. This is how I currently gather that data. I need this additional information—no records I currently keep are producing it.**

In case you haven't heard, there's a handy new machine on the market that can help enormously in converting data into information. It's called a computer. Are you—and your business—ready for one?

I diligently avoided all the new technology until last summer. But, with a teenager in the household for the summer months who continuously babbled about RAMs and ROMs and Ks, my wall of resistance was finally breached.

My fifteen-year-old son John introduced me to computers the easy way—through games. When I objected to the usual shoot-'em-up types, he told me about Frogger. It's a lively game for pacifists like myself in which the player helps five green frogs negotiate the hazards of a highway and stream to finally find safe havens in their swamp. A dumb challenge, maybe, but fun.

John's next step was to get me to visit a computer store. While he elbowed his way to a machine I kept my hands in my pockets. When he reached out to touch the keyboard I hissed, "Don't! You might break it!" He quickly dispelled my fears about the machine's delicacy or his own competence by expertly entering a short program. Then I was ready for books on the subject. Though none had John's colorful explanations, they did add to the base of knowledge he'd given me.

After almost a year of gathering information and getting used to the idea of adding a computer to my life, I have chosen the machine for me. It handles the two programs I need—word processing and data storage. It is also portable—a necessary quality because of the traveling I do for my business.

Most women begin the journey into the world of computers from a point of complete ignorance, as I did. Many of us are "machine suspicious." Most of us have not been extensively trained in math. And both mechanical and mathematical abilities are *assumed* to be necessary for computer competence.

It's just not so! I flunked Algebra II and I'm happily learning how to program in BASIC. I don't know how to fix my computer but I'm not intimidated by its little green screen anymore. I've moved a long way since last summer.

Begin your own computer education today. Talk to your own teenagers. Play computer games. Visit computer stores. Read books. Spend a Saturday at the local computer fair. Talk to other business owners about the computers and programs they use.

Don't be intimidated by complicated language. The only thing a computer can do is convert raw data to usable information. Concentrate on the questions you want to have answered. Then look for ways a computer can help you do it.

24

Can I Use Independent Contractors Rather Than Employees in My Business?

Have you ever considered hiring independent contractors rather than direct employees? Most business owners never consider this alternative. Yet hiring independent contractors, rather than employees, has several advantages.

1. Independent contractors are already experts in their chosen field. You do not spend valuable time training them.
2. Independent contractors are paid only for the tasks they actually accomplish. If they sit around wasting time they pay for it. Not you.
3. Independent contractors are responsible for their own contributions to the Social Security system and for payments for appropriate insurance coverages. You do not have to pay additional labor burden expenses to get a particular job done.
4. Independent contractors are easy to fire. If they don't perform you find someone else who will. Period. No arguments.
5. Independent contractors save paperwork. You file only one document with the federal government for each of them—an end-of-the-year report of compensation over $600. Compare that to paperwork per direct employee!
6. Independent contractors are business owners. You and they share a common set of values.

For all of these reasons, I now hire *only* independent contractors. I hire a bookkeeper to do the bookkeeping. I hire an accountant to do the accounting. I hire an attorney to handle legal matters. I hire a shipper to pack and ship books. I hire a typist to type. I hire a typesetter to typeset, a printer to print, and a binder to bind.

To me, the core of independent contracting is the insistence that a person be paid for a task accomplished. The usual arrangement of paying an employee to occupy a particular piece of geography for a particular duration of time—with little regard for some strict measure of production—has always struck me as being supremely foolish.

At the Treillage Shop, I would have preferred to consider my drapery manufacturers as independent contractors. But, since these women worked regularly at my place of business, federal regulations designated them as direct employees. I did, however, carry over the *spirit* of independent con-tracting.

I paid each employee "by the task." In our case "the task" was a completed width of drapery. An average pair of drapes contains four to eight widths.

This working arrangement produced several surprising results. First, we found we could arrange time much more flexibly. It no longer mattered when an employee was there, as long as her assigned widths were completed by the end of the week.

One woman came in early so she could be back home again when her kids arrived from school. Another slept late in the morning and worked through suppertime. As temperatures rose in July and August, they worked only in the cool of the evening. Occasionally they took work home to complete.

Each employee took a greater pride in her work. Since each had her own widths to complete, no one had to deal with another's mistakes. If errors did occur, I could trace them to the source immediately.

The strict relationship we established between production and pay helped all of us. It enabled me to give firm, correct labor estimates to my customers. It also taught me not to impose on my employees. A phone ringing? It was my job to answer it. Housekeeping? My job too. My em-ployees were being paid to produce completed widths of drapery, not to sweep threads off the floor.

If you have employees, find ways to pay for actual tasks accom-plished rather than for time spent occupying a work space.

Also, consider the benefits of using independent contractors in your business. There are stern federal regulations about who qualifies as an independent contractor. These guidelines are listed in *Circular E—Em-ployer's Tax Guide.* Pick up a copy at your local IRS office.

Yours to Do. Here is a chart of all the different tasks I currently do in my business. I've listed such things as placing orders, arranging floor displays, seeing clients, paying bills. If it is a task *only I can do for my business,* I've checked it off. If someone else can do as well as or better than I, what about hiring an independent contractor? I've noted some possible contractors.

TASKS	ONLY I CAN DO IT	POSSIBLE INDEPENDENT CONTRACTORS

25

Is It Time to Review My Insurance?

As your business grows and changes, so do your insurance needs. Your retail store opened with $5,000 in initial inventory. Since then you have consistently added new lines. Your new inventory level is $7,500. Have you notified your insurance agent to increase fire insurance coverage?

After two years of explosive growth, your manufacturing operation boasts a payroll of seven employees. Have you consulted your insurance agent about a group policy to cover major medical expenses and hospitalization costs?

You have moved your service business from your home to a new location downtown. Have you discussed the possibility of additional insurance with your agent?

Review your insurance program periodically. Make sure coverage remains adequate as you grow.

Yours to Do. I've reviewed all my insurance policies. Here's a list of the types and limits of insurance coverage I now have.

_____

_____

_____

_____

It's obvious I need to make these changes. I'll call my agent today.

_____

_____

_____

_____

_____

_____

_____

26
Am I Working Under
the Right Legal Structure?

There are three legal structures for a business—sole proprietorship, partnership, and corporation. You chose one of these three legal forms when you opened your business. By now you have a couple of years' experience with it.

Sole proprietorship is the simplest and least expensive legal structure. Liability is the only real problem. As a sole proprietor, you and your business are one. What your business owes, you owe *personally*. What your business owns, you own *personally*.

You can run a sole proprietorship without an attorney or an accountant—though I don't advise it. NEVER TRY TO RUN A PARTNERSHIP OR CORPORATION WITHOUT PROFESSIONAL ADVICE. YOU CAN GET YOURSELF INTO BIG TROUBLE.

Most business owners would not consider forming a corporation without legal advice. Those same business owners might form a partnership with only a handshake.

If you want to work with a partner, protect yourself and your investment. Choose your partner carefully. Discuss, in detail, specific responsibilities and put your agreement in writing. Don't just record it on the back of an envelope. Make it a formal, legal document.

A corporation is the third possible legal structure for a business. It is also the least well understood. The most time-consuming. The most expensive. And the most mysterious.

According to an 1819 decision by Chief Justice John Marshall, a corporation "is an artificial being, invisible, intangible, and existing only in contemplation of the law." In effect, a corporation is a legal entity that is distinct and separate from the individuals who own it. It can make contracts, sell or buy property, and negotiate loans. Unless there are some very special reasons—such as a real need to limit an owner's personal liability—a corporation is generally more hassle than it's worth.

Corporation structures attract business owners who are interested in sheltering income. For a business with a net profit over $50,000, a corporation may supply some tax advantages.

But recent changes in federal tax law give a sole proprietor equal opportunity to shelter income in a Keogh Plan. In 1984 a sole proprietor may put as much as 20% of her net business income—maximum annual contribution $30,000—into a Keogh Plan. The amount you contribute is deducted from this year's taxable income, thereby reducing both tax bracket and tax bill. Such tax-deferred contributions, wisely invested, can build a sizable nest egg for later years.

Consult both your attorney and your accountant when contemplating any change in your legal structure. Lack of advice now can cause lots of grief later.

Yours to Do. **Am I satisfied with my current legal structure?** _____

What alternative structures am I considering? _____

_____

Whose professional advice have I sought regarding these alternatives? _____

_____

_____

As a sole proprietor, did I contribute to a Keogh Plan last year? ____

How much? _____

How much do I plan to contribute this year? _____

If you have not yet investigated the tax benefits of a Keogh Plan, do it today! Don't pay more taxes on your hard-earned money than you absolutely have to.

27

How Do I Want
My Business to Expand?

Sometimes business growth comes in small steps. Sometimes it comes in leaps and bounds. Small steps are gradual expansion of the number of hours you are available to customers or a gradual increase in inventory levels. Opening a new shop across town or developing two new products for market are examples of large leaps of expansion. Both kinds of growth require planning.

Of course, your business can grow without a plan, but the process will be haphazard and uncertain. A master plan for growth gives you not only a sense of direction but also some goals to shoot for. It also lets you anticipate one of the biggest problems in any business—positive cash flow.

Unforeseen expansion can be as big a problem as an unexpected drop in sales. Both put your business in the same position—strapped for cash.

A banker prefers seeing you for a leisurely lunch during which you explain anticipated money needs six months hence. It gives you both the chance to get used to the idea. The alternative—a frazzled session to humbly request sufficient funds to avoid a disconnect on your telephone— is a horrid experience.

Learn the benefits of planning. Give yourself a chance to solve problems before they occur. Of course you will never discover and solve every problem. But next winter your business will not hand you a double load of trouble *if* you take the time now to cut that load in half by planning.

Use the planning chart to project this year's business expansion. You'll find it almost as exciting as planning a new business—with one important exception: you now have two years' business experience and wisdom to help.

***Yours to Do.* Record sales projections and requirements for new capital in the income section at the top of the chart. Record projected production and operating expenses at the bottom of the chart. Carry total income and total expenses to the middle of the chart and figure your cash flow position.**

MONTH / YEAR	1	2	3	4
INCOME				
NEW CAPITAL				
SALES				
1				
2				
3				
TOTAL INCOME				
CASH FLOW				
TOTAL INCOME				
TOTAL EXPENSES				
MONTH'S END CASH				
CUMULATIVE CASH ON HAND				
EXPENSES				
PRODUCTION				
1				
2				
3				
4				
5				
6				
OPERATING				
1				
2				
3				
4				
5				
6				
7				
8				
9				
10				
TOTAL EXPENSES				

5	6	7	8	9	10	11	12

28

Where Will I Get the Money to Expand My Business?

Getting money to start a business is one matter. Getting money to expand a business is another.

My brother Tom runs a manufacturing operation. He and a partner refine sugar for pharmaceutical uses. When they started the business three years ago they made the usual frustrating rounds of local bankers. And heard the usual discouraging answer—no. Great idea but no business history. They finally managed to raise the required capital by enlisting a silent partner.

Last year, in need of expansion funds, they reapproached a banker. Laden with cash flow projections, income statements, and balance sheets, they were fully armed for a convincing presentation. The banker greeted them cordially. After a handshake and a reminder about their previous meeting Tom proceeded with his well-prepared facts and figures. Halfway through the banker interrupted: "Looks good. How much do you need?" Surprised, Tom stated a sum.

While completing the loan arrangements Tom asked the banker about his change in attitude. Leaning back in his swivel chair, the banker said, "Three years ago you came in here and told me you were going to do something. Today you came in and told me you've done it. There's a big difference between the ones who say they're going to do it and the ones who have actually gone and done it."

How very true!

Two years ago you fell into the banker's first category. You were a person with high hopes of doing something. By now you've moved into category two. You've gone and done it. Over the last couple of years you've acquired another very important business asset. A track record.

Raising money to expand a business won't be a piece of cake but it's much easier than borrowing money to start a business. Bankers, friends, or business associates aren't naive. They still want assurance their capital investment or loan will be secure. And they want concrete information to prove it. But you've come a long way in the last two years—from having a dream to making a dream come true. You've proved you can do it. And that counts for a lot.

Approach any money source with a sense of self-esteem and appreciation for what you've done. Arm yourself with the facts and figures you've accumulated about your past history and future prospects. Negotiate enthusiastically for the expansion of your dream.

Yours to Do. Before I approach any source for money, I *promise* I will spend some time reviewing how far I've come since I started my business.

Then I will check to see that I have copies of the following documents for my presentation.

Income Statement	_____	Income/Expense/Cash Flow Statement for the next twelve months	_____
Balance Sheet	_____	Market Plan	_____
Break-even Chart	_____	Chart of Sales for each year in business	_____

PART FOUR

CONSULTING THE EXPERTS

Eleven Women Who Are Running Their Businesses Successfully

Elizabeth Bertani and Pat Sherwood, Parsley Patch, Santa Rosa, California

Pat Sherwood and Elizabeth Bertani are both vegetarians. Finding a lack of natural gourmet seasonings on the market, they decided to produce their own. Their original idea has expanded rapidly over the last two years.

Me: How did Parsley Patch start? Why did you choose herb and spice blends?

Pat: Each of us spent seventeen years in the kitchen. Cooking and preparing food are both something we like to do and gifts we like to offer. Elizabeth formulated the all-purpose blend and passed it around to friends. They told her, "This is so good it should be on the market."

Elizabeth: Pat and I attended a weekend workshop together about two and a half years ago. During a lunch break we sat on the lawn at Sonoma State University and talked about what we wanted to do with our lives.

We both wanted to go to graduate school. Pat was interested in writing fiction. I wanted to write nutritional documents. "Look," I said, "let's take this spice blend, name it, label it, start a little business, and sell the stuff. With the proceeds we'll be able to send ourselves to graduate school."

Pat: You know, we started out with $5,000 and were convinced that that amount would launch our product. I suppose our naiveté was a benefit. Had we known the amount of money we would really need, we would have been frozen with fear.

Me: How are things different than you expected?

Elizabeth: Initially, we were very naive. We thought that you start a business, sell the product, take the money, and go home. We also thought that we'd make money instantly!

Things snowballed. We started with an idea of one blend in a cute, funky little jar with a homespun label. We ended up with seven blends instead of one, an expensive designer for our label, a warehouse, machinery, and eight employees.

Pat: Our original target market was specialty food stores, organic groceries, and giftware shops—all in Sonoma County.

Elizabeth: Almost immediately we started selling nationally through contacts we made at trade shows. We hired sales representatives who worked on commission in other areas of the country. By our first summer, when we had been selling three months, we had distribution in eight other states.

We also found, early on, that our work assignments were unrealistic. Initially we set up a division of labor with Pat doing the books and office work. I worked in the warehouse doing the blends. We both sold the products.

Pat, with her seven years' banking experience, was much more sophisticated than I, financially. When someone said "money" I hid my head. I just wanted the money to spend so I could do my advertising and make my blends. Pat had to put up with a lot of resistance to my learning the money side of the business. I'm just now beginning to feel comfortable discussing financial things. But, to keep the company growing, I now know I have to help Pat share that burden.

Looking back over these past two years, we feel like snakes who have outgrown our skins.

Pat: As we outgrew some of our initial systems we got help. We ferreted out people who had excellent reputations in their own businesses. We took them to lunch and told them we wanted to pick their brains. We asked them lots of questions in their specific areas of expertise. We can never put a dollar value on the free advice we asked for and received.

Me: What's your experience been with bankers?

Pat: I had a fifteen-year history with our banker. That established relationship really helped us in the beginning.

Money has always been a scramble for us. We look back now at some of the loans we've gotten and they seem foolish in retrospect. But you do what you have to do at the moment just to keep things going.

We thought that after two years this company would be able to stand on its own and we could borrow without using our homes as collateral. It hasn't happened yet.

Elizabeth: I can't state strongly enough how easy it is to underestimate money needs. It's a very typical mistake of young businesses—and a primary reason why small businesses fail. Expenses will always be at least twice what you imagine.

Me: Is your partnership still working well after these first two years?

Elizabeth: Yes. Pat and I work well together. If we make a mistake we don't worry about being rejected. I think it gets down to unconditional acceptance of each other. It's like a marriage.

We find that one ingredient is absolutely essential: complete honesty. We are confident that it's all right to disagree with each other, to want to do something in a different way, to feel upset or angry. We say what we mean. We don't keep hidden agendas.

For Pat and me, working together is a cooperative effort. That same ethic extends to our employees. We work with each other. Our employees also work with us—not for us.

Pat: Women are natural caretakers, they want everyone around them *tucked in and taken care of. Because we express this female trait in our business, our employees are extremely loyal.*

Elizabeth: *We get an incredible quality of work from our people. They constantly think how they can improve their own work capacity and the business in general. Pat and I never keep appreciation to ourselves. We share it with our employees. We don't say, "I did it." We say, "We did it."*

Me: Have you made a lot of mistakes?

Elizabeth: *We have made so many mistakes! We feel that they were all due to insufficient information at the time. But we've evolved and learned. We don't waste time or energy worrying about the money we've wasted or the wrong selling approaches we've used.*

Me: Has any large company approached you to buy Parsley Patch?

Elizabeth: *Yes, we do have inquiries. There are small companies like ours who do sell out on a contractual basis—an up-front investment and relinquish control five years from the date of the agreement. And some owners sell their companies totally and stay on to manage. In both cases, you give up control of decisions and lose your autonomy.*

Pat: *We have decided to oversee the growth of Parsley Patch ourselves. It has become a tremendous learning arena for all of us—Elizabeth, myself, and our employees. We have a commitment to ourselves and to them to develop our fullest potential, not only professionally but personally.*

Me: How has being businesswomen affected your families?

Pat: *I've noticed a change in my son. He'll say, "When I grow up I'll start a business doing this." He's always looking for things that haven't been done. He knows it's not impossible—that he can do it!*

Elizabeth: *Balancing personal and professional lives is a constant challenge. But now I'm respected for being a businesswoman and a mother. Male and female family members help clean the house and take out the garbage. In my family we are breaking the traditional roles according to which boys grow up to be men who read the newspaper and mow the lawn and girls grow up to be mothers who cook.*

Beverly Mathews, Bed and Breakfast, Los Angeles, California

Beverly Mathews conveys warmth and caring as she describes her busy life. Grown children, an actor husband, a menagerie of pets, a stream of guests to her bed and breakfast home—none of them faze this talented woman.

Me: Do you run your bed and breakfast business as a full-time operation?
Beverly: No. Right now I am working as a production coordinator on a television "Movie of the Week." And on Saturdays I give seminars about how to get into the bed and breakfast movement, as well as starting other home-based businesses.

I didn't want to start a large-scale inn and sink hundreds of thousands of dollars into debt. I don't think that's the way to start. I might find I hated it. Or the romance might disappear with eighteen-hour days and making beds for guests. I'm doing it on a small scale, in my home, as a sideline business.
Me: How did you get started?
Beverly: I opened my home as a bed and breakfast after returning to California from the East Coast. I used to be an actress, and my husband had roles on Broadway and in soap operas so we lived there for a while.

When we moved back to Los Angeles, in 1976, I didn't want to go back into acting. I wanted to be more responsible for my own life—and I was willing to give up money to do so. I cut back on things that I felt were not important.

We have a beautiful home. It's even been used as a movie location. We've remodeled it ourselves. We've done our own upholstery and quilts.

I answered a small ad in Sunset *magazine. It was placed by a woman who was starting a B & B organization. She was looking for people who had homes they were willing to share with guests. She formed an organization of private memberships—both hosts and guests. Each person knows something about all the others in the organization so no one is a total stranger.*

Hers is only one of hundreds of such organizations all over the country. Some are private membership types where you pay annual dues and a percentage of the room fee. Others are merely referral services. I belong to several different groups.

You have no idea how big this movement is. As Americans become more trusting and willing to meet people from other countries, bed and breakfast homes such as mine could provide rooms in an area equivalent to the number of rooms in a large hotel!

Most people my age have a room or two they can use to produce additional income. You don't need a big old house, just a few bedrooms.

Me: How does running a bed and breakfast fit in with your family life?

Beverly: *My children find it fascinating. My husband finds it fun if it's convenient. Or a pain in the neck if it isn't convenient. He's an actor and, if he does a play and comes home at two in the morning, he wants to roam around the house. Not easy with guests in the house.*

I have four children and they're gradually leaving home—though not as fast as I expected. They keep coming back. I have to know ahead of time if I need a room for one of them or I can use it for a B & B guest.

Every once in a while one of us feels our privacy is being invaded. We say, "No more guests for a while." Then, after we're rested, we go back to it again.

Me: Do you ever turn down guests?

Beverly: *Yes. I don't take single men because I have a teenage daughter. I don't take smokers because I finally quit after all these years.*

Sales people who are on the road love to stay in bed and breakfast homes. They find it quite a relief to stay in a comfortable home as long as they can use a phone in the morning to do their calling. They are not a big part of my clientele but they are in the bed and breakfast movement.

Ours is a lively household. I try to warn guests they shouldn't come here looking for total rest. Our guests often serve themselves breakfast and they always make their own beds.

Me: Do you have help with the house—a housekeeper or a cleaning lady?

Beverly: *The idea of a housekeeper appalls me. I know that five minutes later, with our crazy lifestyle, everything will be a mess again. I've learned to make our house appear beautiful myself in about twenty minutes . . . just don't open the closets.*

I'm very organized and a great maker of lists. I don't always finish my list but I carry parts over to the next day. And I always do the thing I like least first.

Me: Tell me how you're expanding on your original business idea.

Beverly: *Now that I am somewhat of an authority on how to start and run a bed and breakfast, I have started to teach others how to do it via seminars and telephone/mail counseling that can reach anyone who comes and attends the local workshops.*

A wide variety of people are attracted to my classes. Some want to get out of the rat race and do something for themselves. They are more concerned with a change of lifestyle than with making a lot of money. Some people are preparing for retirement, have a house, and want to rent out their extra rooms.

It's very exciting to know I've helped so many people—especially women—to increase their self-esteem. I feel very strongly about women's starting to take control of their own lives. I have found that if you do something yourself, no matter how tiny, it makes you feel more worth while. Most women feel trapped at home and just don't see what they have to offer. I'm teaching them how to use their homes as income producers . . . trying to get the best of both worlds!

I have put together a lot of materials that I send home with people in my seminars—information on zoning, insurance requirements, safety factors, legal considerations, referral organizations, the personal approach to promotion that I've used so successfully. I'm seriously considering writing a book. I could suggest what to serve, how to serve, how to treat people.

I've already cowritten a book on bargain shopping while I was back East. It's now in its fifth printing. My partner and I marketed it ourselves and did all the public relations work. In fact, the New York Times once did a half-page story on it, my family, and our lifestyle.

I am also an adviser—currently unpaid—to a newly formed company. They found me through my seminars. They have offered me a position traveling throughout the country giving seminars as I do here. I haven't given them an answer yet. I don't know if it's something I'd like to do, since my home life is terribly important to me.

Diane Worthington, Zoftig, San Francisco, California

Diane Worthington formed her business to solve a personal problem. Always a large woman, she wanted comfortable, fashionable clothes. Zoftig, her San Francisco retail shop for large-size women, solves the problem not only for herself but for lots of other women besides.

Me: Why did you start a business to sell clothing to large-size women?
Diane: I've been a large woman all my life and I've always found it difficult to find good clothes in my size. I had a dream of opening my own store for at least fifteen years. It took me that long to get the experience and financing together. Why someone else hadn't done it in the meantime I'll never know.

Market research shows that the adult population of the United States in size 16 or over spends five to seven billion dollars a year on clothes. It's a large segment of the population that has always been ignored.

I always wanted to be a stylish dresser. I learned early that if I am forced to dress in black polyester I am going to be a depressed person. But if I dress well I will get respect no matter what size I am.
Me: I understand you started in mail order.
Diane: Yes. I started doing mail order from my dining-room table. Later I converted a bedroom into an office. I sold a very limited line of moderately priced large women's clothing.

I sent out a questionnaire to every woman who responded to my ads. I asked them what they wanted in large-size clothing, what fabrics they preferred, what fitting problems they had. Answers came back by the thousands. Women would even write or draw pictures on the back of the questionnaire. I compiled a lot of information that way.

I have no formal training in retail merchandising. This has always been a seat-of-the-pants kind of operation. I began with a gut-level feeling of what the market demanded. When I ferreted out expert sources of market research they supported my ideas.

While the mail-order business did not make me a fortune, it was a really good way to cut my teeth in the clothing business—to get the education and background I needed. While mail order could become a very lucrative business, I found that it didn't satisfy my need for personal contact. In order to be really happy in business I needed to get out and deal

*with designers and manufacturers. Saying hello to customers is impor-
tant to me. So is throwing parties in the store. I want the personal feed-
back.*

Me: How did you finance your expansion from mail order to a store?

Diane: *That's a really interesting story. I didn't go to a bank because my
husband was a medical student. We were living on grants and loans. Instead I approached a personal friend who is rather well off.*

*I asked him over one night to take a look at a vacant metal shop that
would be a perfect location for my store. I just started talking about my
vision of the place. My enthusiasm was infectious because I believed so
firmly in the project. He jumped right in, said yes, and told me he didn't
see how I could fail.*

*Actually, I took out my first bank loan just last year—a short-term in-
ventory loan for the Christmas season. By that time I had such a history
of large deposits at the bank that the manager gave me a loan just on
my word.*

Me: Did you have a grand opening for the shop?

Diane: *We sure did! I keep a working mailing list from the mail-order
business. We sent out 1,600 invitations. Five hundred people showed up
the first day. We gave away gifts and served champagne.*

*Before that day, my staff had never written a sales slip, called for
authorization on a credit card, or gift-wrapped a package. But everyone
wanted us to succeed. We had a ball.*

Me: What lines do you carry in the shop?

Diane: *Everything except foundation garments. We have sportswear,
business dresses, cocktail dresses, a limited line of shoes, and beautiful
accessories. We also have a special line of designer pieces.*

*I sent out a letter to clothes designers in the San Francisco area ask-
ing them to join this project and design for larger women. I found a hand-
ful who really understand what large women need—comfortable live-in
clothing and also exquisite one-of-a-kind designer pieces, quilted, hand-
painted silks, that last and can be purchased for a good price. I now
carry clothes from twenty-five such designers at Zoftig.*

*Men visit the store and go straight to the lingerie rack. We always
have coffee and a cheese tray and try to make them comfortable. We
also model garments if they wish. I feel very satisfied with the work we
do.*

Me: Has your competition changed since you opened?

Diane: *When I opened there was very little competition. It was a heart-
breaking experience for a large woman to shop. The comments I used
to hear galled me. And there were no large saleswomen either.*

*Now there are new boutiques opening all the time. There's a whole
renaissance of thinking in the market about the large woman. I shop the
competition and find that there is plenty of room for all of us.*

*On the other hand, it's wonderful to be the first. I think anyone with
a unique idea for a business should jump right in and do it.*

Me: What important lessons have you learned during these first couple of years?

Diane: People who go into business and don't set aside an advertising budget really make a mistake. You can have the greatest product in the world but if people don't know about it they won't beat a path to your door. One of the best decisions I made when I opened Zoftig was to hire a publicist. I pay her a retainer and she creates news stories for me. She has paid for herself fifty times over by getting stories placed in magazines and on TV.

I also learned the value of going to apparel mart shows. While doing mail order, I learned a lot about form, line, fabric, and fabrication. I've expanded my knowledge tremendously by going to the market show five times a year. I meet manufacturers, see what they are selling, see their mistakes.

And personnel, that was a big area for me. I thought you just hired someone and everything would be hunky-dory. That's not always so.

I now have a staff of three and I can leave the store and delegate authority and be comfortable. I am a demanding boss, but I pay a good wage and my employees love the business.

We are all on the same wavelength. I don't mind telling you, Zoftig is a large-woman-owned and large-woman-operated business. Myself and my employees are the best advertisements we have.

Me: How does your family life fit in with running a business?

Diane: It's a unique situation because my store is just a few doors from my home. My kids, who are eleven, twelve, and fourteen, don't quite understand that the shop is not the place to discuss a special problem with Mom.

I have taken on help with running the house. But I still love to be a homemaker and take great pleasure in my home, my children and pets— including a new Newfoundland puppy.

My husband finishes his medical education in June. He's now an intern with wild hours. But we do make time for the family.

Me: What are your plans for growth?

Diane: I recently received an offer from a large retail store that wants to incorporate Zoftig into its downtown San Francisco store. The management would let me keep complete control. I was flattered by the offer but scared, too, because of the competition. I've decided to stay here instead and continue to create the kind of store I always wanted to shop in.

Janet Fischer, New Homes, Inc., St. Paul, Minnesota

Janet Fischer formed New Homes, Inc., over twelve years ago to serve the house-marketing needs of the Minneapolis-St. Paul area. Since then the business has evolved into four separate divisions—all of which Janet still supervises.

Me: What do you do at New Homes, Inc.?
Janet: New Homes, Inc., is an overall name for my company. We deal with various aspects of housing marketing. Essentially, there are four divisions.

*One company, JMF Advertising, concentrates on advertising. A second company puts out two publications—*New Homes *magazine, which is directed to consumers, and* New Homes Financial Letter, *which is directed to real estate professionals. Both of these companies have been in operation over ten years.*

Two and a half years ago we added a third business operation, a real estate brokerage. It's not a significant part of the business yet. But it's a logical growth area. We will be concentrating on new housing developments and condominium conversions.

More recently, I have formed an affiliate company that is actually a partnership. We've handed over to it two areas of business formerly handled by JMF Advertising—market research and feasibility studies.

We have found that separate services are more salable. It's easier to sell a client one service from one company rather than lots of services from one company.
Me: You started JMF Advertising in 1971, didn't you?
Janet: Yes. When I started twelve years ago it was unusual for women to have their own businesses. I was $400 in debt when I started. I went to my banker to borrow enough money to buy a desk and a typewriter—about $800—and this fellow looked at me in a condescending manner and said, "We will need a cash flow statement. Your husband will know what that is!"
Me: How were your early years in business?
Janet: Difficult because of personal events, but I was doing what I wanted to do—piloting my own ship. Three months after I opened JMF I was pregnant with my first child. Three months after the baby was born my

106

mother died very suddenly. Three months after that my brother-in-law was killed in a plane crash. A year later my second child was born.

During those years of personal crisis I managed to start two businesses. I was physically exhausted; emotionally, I felt totally numb. But I kept on going. I never really considered anything else or that I wouldn't succeed. If I had stopped to worry about whether I would or wouldn't succeed—chances are I would have failed.

Me: Do you do a lot of advertising for your own companies?

Janet: *No, not in a formal sense, except that we do advertise JMF Advertising in* New Homes *magazine since our audience is so closely matched to our magazine distribution.*

Mostly we concentrate on promotion. We generate a lot of inquiries from people because of our professional affiliations. I'm a member of the National Association of Homebuilders, the Minnesota Homebuilders, and two city homebuilders' associations, as well as the apartment associations from the local to the national level. We go to all of their meetings. People know us and what we do.

This kind of exposure has done far more for us than any advertising. It might not be fair to say that other kinds of advertising wouldn't work. I just haven't done it.

Me: How many people do you employ?

Janet: *There are usually eight to ten people on staff, including me. We also use a lot of free-lancers—writers, artists, and designers for the magazine and for our ads.*

We have become very self-sufficient with a small core of people who put out a lot of work. I arranged it this way because the work load is seasonal, extremely cyclical, and extremely volatile. One of the most difficult things in a business like this is to recognize the need to cut back on staff and overhead expenses.

Nineteen eighty-one and 1982 were absolute disasters. Our bad debt rate, alone, was unbelievable. The business began taking off again as interest rates lowered. I'm always wary of things expanding too quickly. A rapid increase in sales drives housing prices up. That's just as destructive as high interest rates.

Me: Do you use the services of an accountant and an attorney?

Janet: *Yes. I believe both services are absolutely necessary. It is money well spent.*

I got very good advice from my first attorney. However, he was a member of a very large law firm and my company just didn't fit into his clientele.

The attorney I have now is absolutely great. He is crisp and I really like him. He is also patient when I pay slowly and I appreciate that.

I think the biggest failing of attorneys is their lack of follow-through. You need to keep reminding them to perform. Most of them are just terrible.

Me: Have you had any problems balancing your business and family life?

Janet: *Of course. I was married for seven and a half years before I had* *any children and I highly recommend it. I don't agree that you should have kids when you're very young.*

I chose to start a business instead. I started it while I still had the guts and confidence to try. I was too young or too naive to realize I might not succeed.

I'm where I belong—in business. I sincerely like to run things. I like to be in charge. I like to get things done. I want to be in control. The longer I'm in business the more I realize that.

Me: Did you make any major mistakes during the first two years of your business?

Janet: *None that were fatal. I do seem to repeat the same mistakes over and over, but they don't throw me anymore—and the degree of goof is less—and I do learn from them.*

Looking back, I should have taken a course in management. I had no management experience and that really hurt. But instinctively, I think, I manage people pretty well. We have an excellent attitude and support system within our staff. All of us believe very strongly in what we're doing.

I'm in the process now of reading In Search of Excellence. *It's a wonderful book. Every woman should read it. It describes how great corporations in their definition are managed—the same way a woman in-*stinctively *manages people.*

Ann Dwyer, California Rivers, Geyserville, California

A sudden life change propelled Ann Dwyer into business. She turned a longtime interest in canoes into California Rivers—a business that sponsors river trips and manufactures river-running equipment.

Me: What did you do before California Rivers?
Ann: I was a fairly typical housewife—mother of four children, husband climbing the corporate ladder, volunteer activities. BUT I also taught swimming as a Red Cross instructor. That led me to canoeing and to my present business.
Me: What changed you from a housewife to a business owner?
Ann: Actually, it was a divorce. After my divorce I considered what I wanted to do. Real estate was a choice. I probably would be wealthy now if I had gone that route. But I would never have received the satisfaction I'm receiving from developing a business and using my creative talents.

I had formed the Marin Canoe Club and led Sierra Club national outing Family Canoe trips while I was still married. The first Sierra Club Family Canoe trip was on lakes in northern Minnesota. By leading a trip there I hoped to learn about the best equipment for canoe tripping.

After using available equipment for a week, I felt I could make many improvements and started developing river-running equipment that was lightweight, waterproof, and easy to handle.

I had actually designed and made my first waterproof river bag about two years earlier, so I was far more critical about the equipment than the average canoeist.

The next year I made a set of bags for the food and commissary gear for the trip. Those first commercial bags were made at home. Requests came from canoeing friends for their own waterproof bags and made me think I should consider this as a serious venture, so I contacted commercial raft companies to generate interest.
Me: California Rivers is a collection of different operations, isn't it?
Ann: Yes. Our primary operation is manufacturing. We produce a line called Dragonfly Design products, primarily for canoeing, kayaking, and river rafting, which I wholesale all over the United States and in some foreign countries. California Rivers also operates a small retail store in

Geyserville, California, which specializes in the sale of canoes and Kiwi kayaks. I also have a retail mail-order catalogue. The company also offers deluxe canoe and Kiwi kayak trips.

Connected to California Rivers are Osprey Advertising, which handles our advertising operations, and GBH Press, which publishes our books.

There is also AN/CO—Ann's Cooperative Adventures International—a nonprofit operation. It gives me an opportunity to plan and run foreign river trips for small groups. These trips are cooperative, not profitmaking. I estimate the costs and do the bookings. After the trip, if there is money left over, it goes back to the tour members. I recently led such trips to New Zealand and Australia.

I purposely set the company up with different independent operations so that I would have the option of selling a part if I got a purchase offer.

Me: *How do you market your various operations?*

Ann: *Our manufactured products are advertised in specialty and trade magazines. We also exhibit them at trade shows. The mailing list for our retail mail-order operation comes from specialized magazines such as* Canoe *and* River Runner. *We market the river trips through magazines like* Sunset, *in local newspapers, and an exhibit at the San Francisco Sports and Boat Show.*

Me: *What was your biggest problem during the first two years?*

Ann: *Developing confidence in my products. Realizing that they were good and that I did have something to offer.*

I'm not following in anyone's footsteps. I am an innovator. And as an innovator with different products, I had to do more selling.

I've been from the top to the bottom and back up again. I get scared sometimes but I'm having a fantastic time. I love putting it all together. But it's not without risk and high stress.

Me: *Have you always been a risk taker?*

Ann: *Yes. I have always said, "Why not give it a try?" I've been an innovator from the time I was very young. Rather than playing with dolls, I designed and made doll clothes. I was the one who organized and planned picnics and parties. When I was thirteen I wanted to take some friends to my family's beach cabin. I planned and organized the entire thing—food, transportation, and the chaperones my mother insisted on.*

Me: *You have grown children. How do they feel about your business?*

Ann: *I've seen a wonderful turnaround on the part of my children, especially my sons. In my marriage, I was nothing but a woman. "Get thee hence to the kitchen, woman," pretty well sums up how I was treated. That's why there is no more marriage. I felt I was worthy of more than that.*

Since I founded California Rivers, I've seen my sons' attitudes change. Now they look at me as a person who is every bit as capable as their father.

All four of my children have worked for me at one time or another even though they all have their own jobs. While I was on a recent trip my older daughter ran the whole California Rivers operation. My other daughter used to sew for me and has led river trips. My older son has run the retail store and my younger son came on a canoe trip last year. They are all very interested and involved with the business.

Me: What do you want to do with California Rivers this year?

Ann: *I want to analyze each of the operations—retail, mail order, manufacturing, trips, and classes. I need to find out which ones are actually the most profitable.*

I'm losing interest in the retail operation. It's a lot of busy work. If I find out that it is not moving as fast as the other operations I'll let it go and concentrate on the others. I am very interested in finding out where my God-given skills are put to best use.

Nilda Zulueta, Aliart Jewelers, Inc., New York, New York

In the twenty years since she left Cuba, Nilda Zulueta has progressed from doing secretarial work for someone else to being the president of her own company. Aliart Jewelers, Inc., is one of the few women-owned gold jewelry manufacturers in the country.

Me: What kind of jewelry do you manufacture at Aliart?
Nilda: *My main business is special orders right now—one-of-a-kind pieces. This is something no one wants to do anymore. I really like to do it. It gives me a chance to look at old pieces and see how they were made. I work in gold and precious stones. Our jewelry prices range from $500 to $8,000.*

We sell only to very fine stores. Right now we have two sales reps—a man who handles New York City for us, and a lady who handles upper New York State and down to the Carolinas.

I started in 1978 with much less expensive pieces—small gold chains and bracelets and cheap beads. In 1980, I started to improve the line and get into better pieces. We've been upgrading it each year since then.
Me: Did it take a lot of money to start your jewelry business?
Nilda: *I started with three people. We each put in $10,000, and that year we made $50,000. I didn't draw a salary for that first year. Only my brother drew a very small salary—just enough to provide.*

We also had a credit line with a bank. The bank started the line of credit with $10,000 and it has now been increased to $125,000.

In 1980, when the price of gold went up, business continued to be very good for us. That line of credit helped us when we started to improve our line.
Me: Do you have a background in jewelry manufacturing?
Nilda: *Yes. I came from Cuba right after Castro took over in 1962. My beginning in this country was in a doll factory.*

From there I went to work for a jewelry manufacturer for $65 a week as an office girl. I started taking care of the shop. Five years before I left, I was made vice-president in charge of operations.
Me: Why did you decide to give it up and start your own business?
Nilda: *Number one, I think I am a very ambitious person. And, number two, I felt that while I was working for some one else I didn't get the rec-*

ognition I deserved. *Taking care of the shop saved my employer $25,000 and all I got was a pat on the back and a thank you.*

I am from Cuba. I am a woman. So you know it was very difficult for me. But so far things have been very good for us. By the end of our 1983 fiscal year we were close to one million dollars in sales.

Me: You seem very knowledgeable about facts and figures. Have you always been interested in that side of business?

Nilda: *No. When I started the business I only cared for the creative part of it. I didn't want to sit down with the accountant. I didn't want to talk with lawyers. All I wanted to do was to create. See a piece finished. Admire it. Like it. If I didn't like it I'd break it up and start over again.*

Then I started attending seminars. I learned the importance of sitting down with lawyers, knowing how to read a financial statement, being able to ask bank officers for more money. I have learned a lot with the training I've received.

Me: Do you have any employees?

Nilda: *Yes. We have seven people who work for us. Two of them do models from my designs. They work on a free-lance basis.*

I do all the buying and supervise everything. One partner is in charge of the bookkeeping. My brother is in charge of the production end of the business.

We all work long hours—from eight in the morning until eight in the evening, five days a week. Sometimes we come in on Saturday to catch up on paperwork—the messy work at the office.

Me: Do you have a family?

Nilda: *Yes. My husband works in his own business. He imports a line of jewelry mountings from Italy.*

I have a son, nine, and a daughter, twelve. Even though I work long hours we have a very close family relationship. I consider myself a very fit mother. The children come to the office and see how hard we work. What I am accomplishing is going to be for them in the future. In a way, I think they are very proud of me.

Though I work in New York City, I live in New Jersey. It's about a half-hour drive away. We come in very early in the morning and work late to avoid the traffic. I'm usually home by eight o'clock or so.

Me: Did you make any mistakes in your first two years?

Nilda: *Yes. I made a lot of mistakes. And one of the reasons the mistakes happened was that I didn't get any advice from a lawyer or an accountant. I just decided I wanted to go into business. I talked to my friend and my brother and we formed a corporation. But there are a lot of details— such as a lease.*

I made a lot of mistakes but they were not in putting a jewelry line together. I only bought what I needed. I didn't buy things that wouldn't sell.

The mistakes we made have actually been valuable. In the long run, I learned a lot.

Me: Where do you see the business going from here?

Nilda: *This is a very expensive business and I want to remain in control of everything just the way I am now. I want it to grow just a little every year.*

And, to tell you the truth, I want to treat myself a little bit now and then.

Me: Where did the name Aliart come from?

Nilda: *Ten years ago my mother died. Her name was Alicia and her maiden name was Artime. So I combined the first three letters of each name to make Aliart. It is very sentimental. But I regret that she was unable to see what we have been able to do.*

Joanie Gordon, Round & Firm, Santa Rosa, California

Joanie Gordon, an irrepressible mother of three children, admits to having a Type A personality. Round & Firm, the physical fitness program she developed for pregnant women and new moms, began with four women at the local YWCA. Joanie is now considering franchising the concept nationwide.

Me: When did you first have the idea of a fitness program for pregnant women?
Joanie: I first had the idea when I was pregnant with my daughter Jennifer. Although I was an educated and capable person, I was unprepared for the whole range of life-changing circumstances of pregnancy and parenthood.

Jennifer was born in a military hospital in New Jersey. When I asked about childbirth preparation classes, the staff brushed me off with a comment that I must be from California. No one ever mentioned the importance of fitness for the mother and its effect on the child she is carrying or on her preparation for delivery.

Delivery didn't go well. I had no support, no specialized education to prepare me for the birth. I was alone for seven hours of labor. I knew the pregnancy and birth experience could have been better for me—and for a lot of other women. I decided to provide a service that combined fitness and education and offer it to women during their pregnancy and early postpartum time.

I returned to school to become a Certified Childbirth Educator. I ate, slept, drank, read, and researched everything I could get my hands on regarding the role of fitness in pregnancy, labor, delivery, and recuperation period of a new mother.
Me: Where did you give your first class?
Joanie: I started Round & Firm upon my return to California following a divorce and remarriage. I was pregnant with my son David and determined to put my ideas into action.

I negotiated with the YWCA to teach a class. Until that first night, I thought to offer the class as a service. But when I caught the energy, the camaraderie of all the gals in the class, I was inspired. I thought, "Hey, this is fun. It also has business potential. There are so many more preg-

nant women out there who'd love it. I could be on the cover of News-
week!"

The first class had four women. My tape recorder broke down and I
couldn't use music to accompany the exercises. I just talked continuously—and I still do it today. What I say is educational but my style is
more like a comedy act. I have a lot of fun with it—laughing at myself,
teaching the class to laugh at themselves, sharing predicaments we get
ourselves into. I talk constantly about important aspects of pregnancy,
nutrition, infant care, car seats, and lighten up the dissertations with
comments on "thunder thighs," unmatched socks, and runny noses.

A little later I took over an existing YWCA class for pregnant women.
It was called Natal Nautics and had been started shortly before Round
& Firm. Over the next year and a half I formed these two classes into a
well-organized program. We started with 20 women a week. Eighteen
months later we had 350 a week—some swimming, some exercising, some
doing both.

After women had their babies they'd bring them to class and line
them up against the wall in infant seats. The babies would watch as I
taught a class.

I finally left the YWCA after five years because of differences of opinion on how the program should grow. Round & Firm was growing so fast
it couldn't be contained in one location. And there was a tremendous need
for the service elsewhere in the county. I negotiated facility contracts with
organizations to sponsor the program and began a training series for new
instructors.

Me: Where do you find your instructors?

Joanie: Most of them are nurses or educators who have been in my
classes during their pregnancies. I look for women I call "shiners"—women
who can relate to a class in a positive way and draw the participants
together into a mutually supportive, cohesive group. They are few and far
between. These gals have to be both multifaceted and sparkling.

After training a teacher in the techniques of Round & Firm, I set them
up in a facility, provide ongoing support and supervision, instruct them
in important aspects of community support and publicity. They're on their
way! We meet for monthly staff meetings and in-service training. I ask
health care professionals to join us from time to time so we all stay current on new information.

One of my favorite instructors began as a class participant. She didn't
waste time communicating her enthusiasm to a local television station.
And, much to my surprise, we hit the big time with coverage on "Evening
Magazine."

Me: You obviously have wonderful teaching skills. Do you feel you have
good business skills too?

Joanie: Yes. My educational background was focused in management
and physical education. My paid work combined medical and marketing
experiences. In my free time, as I was moving from base to base with
my first husband, I volunteered for a variety of recreational activities—
trampoline classes, lifeguard at summer camps.

Anyone who has taught a successful recreation class knows the importance of good publicity and public relations. My paid experience in marketing helped me set up successful sales strategies. I knew the importance of networking, getting out, and seeking expertise and support.

I have found I am quite good at graphics design. Having made a lot of mistakes, I now know how to do it right. The first flier I did was atrocious. But it got the word out to the community about the classes with the who, what, when information that is so crucial. I still have that flier in my personal museum. On a bleak day it shows me how far I've come.

I have also found that I am not thrilled by making bank deposits, writing checks, and balancing the books.

Me: Did you find it difficult working while your children were very young?

Joanie: Actually, it was ideal when they were little. I took them along with me and set up a business schedule that was compatible with theirs. In other words, we were always home by nap time.

Now that they are five, seven, and eleven—I have another daughter, Rachel, born two years after David—the time demanded by the business is greater. I try to get home by the time they arrive from school, but I usually don't make it. Being my own boss, I do have the flexibility to be here if they are sick. Then they really need their mom.

Me: What are your plans for growth?

Joanie: We have recently made a number of products available at reduced prices to our classes—infant care lambskins, baby front packs, maternity and nursing bras.

We have also developed a New Family Directory with articles, lists of resources, and advertisements of interest to young families. We also hold a yearly extravaganza called the Great Expectation Baby Fair and Family Festival. It's a showcase for community services, merchants, and crafts people, as well as an educational time. We offer seminars throughout the day on pregnancy, parenting, childbearing, and changing family dynamics.

I'm at a real decision point now. Either restrict the growth of Round & Firm to this area only or find an interested investor and franchise the program nationwide. I will be looking for an investor who shares the same vision of the program I do. I see it working in a positive way on a very large scale. It's time to bring in more talent and make it happen.

Ginny Hodgdon, Hodgdon Contracting, Jamaica Plain, Massachusetts

Learning as she went along, Ginny Hodgdon has built a fine business in construction contracting. She concentrates on remodeling and improvements in older homes in Boston's South End.

Me: How did you get into the residential contracting business?
Ginny: *I went through college and got a degree in biology in 1974. After exploring what it was like to work in a laboratory, I realized my heart wasn't in science.*

A friend offered me a job painting apartments and hallways. We also did odd jobs—fixing windows and patching cracks. We split up as partners after about a year. Since then I've been working on my own, doing mostly carpentry.

In the last four years I've taken a lot of courses to upgrade my skills—carpentry, masonry, plumbing. I'm now taking drafting and architectural courses at night school.

One time I took a course in stair building. It cost me $300—and that's a lot of money. But I made it back on one job. And I've made it back many times since. Courses like that are an investment. You meet a lot of other people to learn from.

Me: Did you spend a lot of money starting your business?
Ginny: *No. I got a loan of $1,000 at one time from my parents. At another time I arranged a loan for the same amount with another woman in business. I needed a van. She needed deliveries done. She loaned me the money. I made her deliveries once every week and paid her off at $100 a month. That's the only financing I've ever really had.*

My only major expense has been tools. If I got a job where I needed some additional tools, I just purchased them at that time.

Me: How do you advertise for business?
Ginny: *A variety of ways. When I started out I advertised in a women's newspaper. I also got referrals from a women's construction network in the Boston area.*

I've also taken fliers door to door. That was a tip I picked up from another contractor. And I did get jobs from it, too.

Now about half of my work comes from people I've already worked for. Word of mouth is very important.

I'm now running an ad in a small Boston weekly specifically geared to one section of Boston. It's an area with a lot of old Victorian row houses where I especially enjoy working.

Me: Are you in competition with trade unions?

Ginny: *No. The unions here are pretty much doing only the big high rises. They don't usually get into anything but new building. They don't bother to go after the single-family residential market.*

Besides, there's not much house building going on right now. It's mostly remodeling. It's a good business to be in right now because people can't really afford to build new homes. They remodel instead.

Me: Does it take a great deal of physical strength to do what you're doing?

Ginny: *You have to like to be physically active, but having to be very strong is largely a misconception. It's more a case of knowing how to use your body and learning how to use tools. It's the tools that do the actual work—and many of them are power driven.*

There are a lot of women working in the trades. Those high rises are not put up with people's muscles. They're put up by machines. A woman could well be running one of those cranes.

Me: How has your business changed since you started it?

Ginny: *I started out doing carpentry work. Then, I didn't use many subcontractors.*

Now, I've expanded into doing general contracting and lots of bathrooms. So I'm hiring plumbers and electricians as subcontractors. I hire them and charge my customers 10–15% over what the subs charge me.

Lately I've been doing more design work. A customer will say, "Give me a new kitchen," or "Build me a new loft platform." I have to decide what the customers want the kitchen or loft to look like and how much they are willing to pay. I'm finding the schooling I'm getting in drafting and architecture is extremely valuable. I apply what I learn at night to what I do during the day.

My next step, I hope, will be to start making some money in real estate. Get a bank loan, buy a building, work on it, and then sell it.

Me: What mistakes did you make?

Ginny: *I made a lot of mistakes the first year or two in estimating the costs of a job. So I lost money on jobs. In contracting, you have to give your customer an estimate of the job beforehand. If it's a low price, you get the job. If it's too low to cover all the costs, you can go back to them later and say, "Sorry, I made a mistake," but you can't collect the full amount. I'm doing quite well with estimating now.*

I did one thing early on that is possible but not really advisable. I learned my trade skills as I learned my business skills. It would have been much easier if I had worked longer for someone else—gotten the trade skills and learned how to estimate. It would have been much easier that way. As it was, I put a double weight on myself—learning two sets of skills at once.

Me: Do you have a family?

Ginny: *I'm single. I'd find it hard even to have a roommate right now. For example, I'm on the phone a lot. I have to keep in touch with both the people I'm working for and my subs.*

I own a three-family house and rent out the two other floors. I run my business out of my house. I have the driveway for my truck and the basement and backyard for storage.

Me: Do you find that men customers and women customers react to you differently?

Ginny: *Yes, in a funny way. Generally it's difficult to work for men. They are real skeptical and hire me only for real little jobs.*

On the other hand, there are women who hire me specifically because I'm a woman. They have been ripped off by male contractors who have an attitude similar to car mechanics'—since women don't know anything, they assume they can charge whatever they please and do lousy work. I find women excited to find me in the contracting business. They give me my best opportunities.

Beverly Tanner, Intravest Centaur, Larkspur, California

Bev Tanner is a nationally known investment counselor. While Bev competently handles hundreds of thousands of dollars of clients' money in her Northern California office, Domino, her standard poodle, snoozes comfortably in the corner.

Me: Where did you find such a strange name for your business?
Bev: *The business started with three partners—two men and myself. They suggested the name "Centaur" from the mythological creature, half man and half animal. I didn't care about the name. I just wanted to get on with business. When we decided to incorporate, we found that there was already a Centaur Securities, so we put "Intravest" in front of it.*

The partnership didn't last, by the way. In less than a year I bought out my two partners.
Me: Who were your first clients?
Bev: *My first clients were teachers. I had worked for the California Teachers Association as a sales representative for a little over a year and a half, selling salary-saving tax-shelter plans.*

With my new company, I could offer these same people a variety of investments not limited to tax-sheltered annuities, such as stocks, bonds, and other tax-incentive investments. I was very successful selling. Once people understand why they need such a program, they buy it.

As an investment planner you have to know not only numbers but people. People don't always say what they mean. You must be able to draw them out and get them to understand what they really want. Counseling is a great deal of my business. Like most women, I'm a good listener. That helps a great deal.
Me: Do you have a lot of formal educational training?
Bev: *Yes. I've taken courses at Marin Community College, Golden Gate University, and the University of California. They were all night courses in marketing and finance taken while I held full-time jobs. I don't have a degree but if I added up all the credits I'd probably have enough for one.*

I now serve on two colleges' boards of directors and teach at the college level. I had thought seriously of getting my Masters in business administration but I've come to the conclusion that, if I want an MBA, I'll hire one.

I am licensed in several different areas. I am an insurance broker, stockbroker, real estate broker, and commodities broker. Since I am licensed in so many different areas, I can direct clients according to their needs. I am more objective than a person operating in only a single area.

In addition to owning Intravest Centaur, I also own part of a brokerage company—Planned Investments, Inc., in San Francisco. We employ a hundred registered representatives. I'm not involved in the day-to-day operation. We have other people running the company for us.

Me: Have you always worked in finance?

Bev: *Actually, I worked as a secretary for many years. And those skills came in very handy when I first opened this business. I could type my own letters and handle office procedures with only a part-time high school girl to help.*

One of my most fascinating jobs as a secretary lasted for eleven years. As a girl Friday—which meant that I did everything—I learned the various aspects of running a business.

The business was a holding company for a retail store, a warehouse, an importing firm, a group of manufacturers' representatives, and two manufacturing concerns. Among other things, I participated in introducing new products to the market, dealt with foreign currencies, negotiated bank loans and union contracts. I not only got a taste of managing a business and the uses of money in business, I also learned moves to keep money circulating among various corporations.

Eventually I got bored with the job. When I was offered another position as a labor relations manager for a large company I took it. I enjoyed the "people" work but after a year and a half I really missed my numbers. People are great but they represent never ending problems that remain unsolved. With numbers, when you get to the end of a sheet it balances. People are more complex.

Me: What kind of person are you?

Bev: *I'm very goal oriented and also very independent. I was an only child and grew up with one parent—a mother who worked. By age nine I was on my own. In many ways I didn't have a childhood—unfortunate, but that's the way it was.*

My goal has always been to make money. But that wasn't my major goal and still isn't. I just want to be happy with whatever I'm doing and reap the benefits of my efforts.

I am very persevering. I give something my all and don't give up. I'm a workaholic, which can be either good or bad. I really enjoy working. It's both my vocation and my hobby. My business is so varied, so diversified, so stimulating, it fills all my needs. Though when someone asks, "What else do you want to do?" I answer, "Lie on a beach and read a book."

Me: What were your biggest problems in the first two years?

Bev: *My only problem in the first two years was with my partners. The wife of one of my partners wanted to become part of the business but* *we didn't need her. That created enough friction to break up the partnership. It was a growing stage for me when I bought them out.*

I've always been totally confident about what I'm doing. I've never, never had any regrets about starting this business.

I've moved very slowly and methodically. I didn't rush ahead and dash off in different directions. I went step by step and learned as I went along. My clientele grew as I grew.

Me: Have you made many adjustments in the business as it's grown?

Bev: *Yes. I've come to a point where I no longer give speeches to small groups. I do give courses to larger groups. I really shouldn't spare that time but I find that at the end of each class I am very, very happy. Teaching and lecturing are gratifying to me.*

I now have to say that someone has to have X number of dollars to be able to work with me. I would still love to work with less well off clients but there are other financial planners who can help them just as well. I've outgrown some clients. They have not moved ahead as fast as I have.

When I started the business I wanted to be known and be involved in every possible investment. Since then I have learned to let go and concentrate on only the best. I deal now in only five different mutual funds, fifteen different stocks, and as many real estate shelters.

Me: Do you have a family?

Bev: *I have a husband. No children. Being in business has caused a lot of problems at home. My husband doesn't understand all the hours I put into the business. Even last night, a Sunday, I was in the office till nine o'clock. I just hate to face a deskful of papers on a Monday morning. My husband has a business that is similar to mine but his working style and clientele are very different.*

As well as becoming more organized and reaching new plateaus over the next few years, I want—hopefully—to be able to balance my professional life with my personal life more successfully.

Mary Grunbaum, The Great American Coverup, Dallas, Texas

Mary Grunbaum's The Great American Coverup, in Dallas, is a center of crafts revival. Mary specializes in quilts, both old and new, as well as classes to pass on many craft techniques.

Me: When did you start your business?
Mary: I started in 1972. I'm now in my eleventh year. I was one of the first to generate interest in quilts and quilting.

I was living in New York at the time. I had decided to go back to school to get a degree in teaching. The closer I got to completing the degree the more I realized teaching was not my style.

I really wanted to do something for myself. I was very uncomfortable working for someone else. I wanted my freedom. But I didn't know anything about how to go about it.

I didn't necessarily want a business in quilts, though I've always been interested in textiles. The degree I finally completed at Rutgers was in fine arts and much of my schoolwork was related to textiles.

At the time, the "country look" really hadn't arrived in New York. My husband and I would come down to Texas where my family lives. We'd buy quilts, go back to New York, and sell them. People weren't very sophisticated then about color and design.

Within three months I had a design line of my own. Mostly children's items—crib quilts and pillows. The business sort of popped up and happened quickly.

We expanded our territory and began purchasing quilts, both old and new, throughout the Midwest. We'd travel by car, purchase quilts, and then sell them to specialty shops all over the country. We even went to Europe to sell.

Some of the most salable quilts came from East Texas. Settlers to that area didn't bring a lot of skills with them and the quilts tend to be crude. But East Texas quilts have a very special look all their own. It's very country.

My husband and I actually started this business together. He is a photographer. He documented each quilt we found. We've actually documented over 2,000 but finally stopped photographing everything and became more selective.

My husband and I worked together for the first three years. And nearly killed each other before we decided to separate our businesses. He never sets foot in the store now—and it's a hundred times better.

Me: How large is your store?

Mary: *Actually, we have three stores. Two are located in an older area of Dallas, about a mile and a half from the downtown area. The other shop, which I run with a partner, is in the suburbs.*

One of the shops in Dallas, about 1,200 square feet of space, is devoted entirely to quilting fabrics and supplies. The other store, 3,500 square feet, is only two doors away. There the footage is equally divided between retail space and space for classes.

We stock old quilts and new ones and quilt-related items such as pillows, potholders, wall hangings. I've had to expand beyond patchwork to find items with a good retail turnover. I've also added rag rugs, folk art, wood pieces, and children's items.

The other half of the store is devoted to classes. We give over sixty different classes during the summer months. And some of them are repeated several times. We teach all the basics of several crafts—quilting, appliqué, smocking. And also have classes in special quilt designs such as the house, log cabin, or double wedding ring patterns.

We have several one-time-only classes to teach how to line a basket or make a pillow or crochet a rug. We have a huge following in our stenciling classes. We introduced that craft two years ago.

The nine employees who work here both teach and sell. Only occasionally do I bring in an outside expert.

Me: You mentioned adding items with a good turnover rate. Do your quilts turn over slowly?

Mary: *Yes. I've always had a cash flow problem. I can't have just a store full of quilts. They don't move that fast.*

I really don't know how many times a year they actually turn over. I'm learning a lot more about turnover by putting all our inventory information on computer. I find it fascinating and at the same time it makes me sick. I've been doing this for so long and I've not really known what I've been doing! Obviously, I've done it halfway decently. I'm still in business.

Me: What's your experience been with bankers?

Mary: *I've had some really horrible experiences. I've only found one banker who saw what I was doing and knew I was serious about it. He used to stop by the store to visit. I also felt free to call him for advice.*

He encouraged me to apply for an SBA loan three years ago. The $120,000 I applied for seemed like a huge amount. I went through a great learning process just filling out the loan application. By the time I was finished I'd found solutions to most of my problems. And I probably could have done without the loan.

I didn't realize then one of the pitfalls of an SBA loan. We had to agree not to borrow any other money. That one loan has limited our access to any other credit.

Me: There's a lot of interest in crafts businesses these days. Do women approach you for advice?

Mary: *Yes, frequently. I tell them to find out what they're doing before they jump in.*

Women start crafts businesses because they are fond of the subject matter. But if they want to stay fond of it they'd better take a look at the business side of things too. A crafts business isn't just a pot of spiced tea shared with a customer. It's toilets to scrub and bills to pay.

Also, it's important for crafts people to find their special niche. Everyone thinks in terms of a retail store. That is not always the answer. A better alternative may be to deal wholesale or to limit production only to certain items or to sell only to special clients. There are all kinds of different ways to accomplish the same end.

Me: Do you have children?

Mary: *I have just, at the age of thirty-eight, become a mother. It's changed my whole life. We adopted a baby. He's a year and a half now. And we're in the process of adopting another.*

I now work only three days a week—Wednesday, Thursday, and Friday. The other days I'm off. When I'm here I'm in the office doing whatever needs to be done—the dirty work. I no longer work on the selling floor.

Me: What were your biggest problems during the first couple of years?

Mary: *Looking back now, I don't see a whole lot of problems. Cash flow was always a problem. My husband and I working together was a problem. We were like two bulls in a china closet. Come to think of it, our working relationship was definitely a bigger problem than cash flow.*

PART FIVE

OTHER SOURCES OF INFORMATION

BIBLIOGRAPHY

I love books. Here are some I have enjoyed. This is not meant to be an exhaustive bibliography, just a few suggestions.

Ash, Mary Kay
Mary Kay: The Success Story of America's Most Dynamic Business-woman (New York: Harper & Row, 1981).

Barbec, Barbara
Creative Cash: How to Sell Your Crafts, Needlework, Designs and Know-How (Tucson, Ariz.: H.P. Books, 1981).

Behr, Marion, and Wendy Lazar
Woman Working Home: The Homebased Business Guide and Directory (Edison, N.J.: WWH Press, 1983).

Bolles, Richard N.
What Color Is Your Parachute? (Berkeley, Cal.: Ten Speed Press, 1981).
The Three Boxes of Life (Berkeley, Cal.: Ten Speed Press, 1978).

————, and **Victoria B. Zenoff**
The Quick Job Hunting Map (Berkeley, Cal.: Ten Speed Press, 1976).

Carnegie, Dale
How to Win Friends and Influence People (New York: Pocket Books, 1981). First published in 1937 and still valuable today.
How to Stop Worrying and Start Living (New York: Pocket Books, 1977).

Cohen, Herb
You Can Negotiate Anything (Secaucus, N.J.: Lyle Stuart, 1980).

Cooper, Mildred and Kenneth
Aerobics for Women (New York: Bantam Books, 1973).

Davidson, Peter
Earn Money at Home: Over 100 Ideas for Business Requiring Little or No Capital (New York: McGraw-Hill, 1982).

Deken, Joseph
The Electronic Cottage (New York: William Morrow, 1981). Contains a detailed but understandable explanation of how a computer works.

Delacorte, Toni, et al.
How to Get Free Press: A Do It Yourself Guide to Promote Your Interests, Organization or Business (San Francisco: Harbor Publishing, 1981).

Dible, Donald M.
Up Your Own Organization: A Handbook for the Employed, the Unemployed, and the Self-Employed on How to Start and Finance a New Business (Reston, Va.: Reston Publishing, 1981). Has an exhaustive bibliography at the end of each chapter.

Dowling, Colette
The Cinderella Complex: Women's Hidden Fear of Independence (New York: Summit Books, 1981).

Emery, Stewart
Actualizations: You Don't Have to Rehearse to Be Yourself (Garden City, N.Y.: Doubleday, 1978).

Frost, Ted S.
Where Have All the Woolly Mammoths Gone? A Small Business Survival Manual (Englewood Cliffs, N.J.: Prentice-Hall, 1977). Written by a CPA with a sense of humor.

Fuller, R. Buckminster
Critical Path (New York: St. Martin's Press, 1981).

Greer, Germaine
The Female Eunuch (New York: McGraw-Hill, 1980).

Hewes, Jeremy Joan
Worksteads: Living and Working in the Same Place (Garden City, N.Y.: Doubleday, 1981).

Hollerbach, Lew
A Sixty minute Guide to Microcomputers (Englewood Cliffs, N.J.: Prentice-Hall, 1982). A quick way to achieve computer literacy.

Jessup, Claudia, and Genie Chipps
The Woman's Guide to Starting a Business (New York: Holt, Rinehart, and Winston, 1980).

Kamoroff, Bernard
Small Time Operator: How to Start Your Own Small Business, Keep Your Books, Pay Your Taxes, and Stay Out of Trouble (Laytonville, Cal.: Bell Springs Publishing, 1981).

————, et al.
We Own It: Starting and Managing Coops, Collectives, and Employee Owned Ventures (Laytonville, Cal.: Bell Springs Publishing, 1982).

Lant, Jeffrey
The Unabashed Self-Promoter's Guide (Cambridge, Mass.: JLA Publications, 1983). A detailed road map to success with the media. Expensive and worth every penny.

McCaslin, Barbara, and Patricia McNamara
Be Your Own Boss: A Woman's Guide to Planning and Running Her Own Business (Englewood Cliffs, N.J.: Prentice-Hall, 1980).

McKeever, Michael P.
Start Up Money: How to Finance Your New Small Business (Berkeley, Cal.: Nolo Press, 1984).

McWilliams, Peter
The Personal Computer Book (New York: Ballantine Books, 1983). In my opinion, the best computer book on the market to date.

Mancuso, Joseph
How to Start, Finance, and Manage Your Own Small Business (Englewood Cliffs, N.J.: Prentice-Hall, 1978).

Marcus, Stanley
Minding the Store (Boston: Little, Brown, 1974) and **Quest for the Best** (New York: Viking Press, 1979). The story of the Neiman-Marcus store in Texas. Musts for anyone interested in establishing a specialty retail business.

Maskowitz, Milton, Michael Katz, and Robert Levering, eds.
Everybody's Business: An Almanac (New York: Harper & Row, 1980). How corporate America got started. Packed with delightful business trivia.

Matthaei, Julie
An Economic History of Women in America (New York: Schocken Books, 1983).

May, Rollo
Man's Search for Himself (New York: Dell, 1973).
The Courage to Create (New York: W. W. Norton, 1975).
Love and Will (New York: W. W. Norton, 1969).

Moran, Peg
Invest in Yourself: A Woman's Guide to Starting Her Own Business (Garden City, N.Y.: Doubleday, 1984).

Naisbitt, John
Megatrends: Ten New Directions Transforming Our Lives (New York: Warner Books, 1982).

Nelson, Paula
The Joy of Money: A Contemporary Women's Guide to Financial Freedom (Briarcliff Manor, N.Y.: Stein & Day, 1975).

Pascale, Richard, and Anthony Althos
The Art of Japanese Management (New York: Simon & Schuster, 1981).

Peters, Thomas, and Robert H. Waterman, Jr.
In Search of Excellence: Lessons from America's Best Run Companies (New York: Harper & Row, 1982).

Phillips, Michael, et al.
The Seven Laws of Money (New York: Random House, 1974).

Phillips and Raspberry
Honest Business (New York: Random House, 1981).

Porter, Sylvia
Sylvia Porter's Money Book (Garden City, N.Y.: Doubleday, 1975).
Sylvia Porter's New Money Book for the 80's (New York: Avon Books, 1980).

Rile, Pat
Fabulous Looks: The Magic of Coordinating (Santa Rosa, Cal.: Take a Good Look, 1981). A commonsense guide to wardrobe planning by the owner of a small business.

Ross, Ruth
Prospering Woman (Mill Valley, Cal.: Whatever Publishing, 1982). A thoughtful presentation of the myths and realities of prosperity.

Rubin, Theodore Isaac
Compassion and Self-Hate (New York: Ballantine Books, 1976). I think this is the most important self-help book on the market today.

Schumacher, E. F.
Small Is Beautiful: Economics as If People Mattered (New York: Harper & Row, 1975).

Scott, Dru
How to Put More Time in Your Life (New York: Rawson Wade, 1980). Practical book on time management.

Segal, Hillel, and Jesse Berst
How to Select Your Small Computer . . . Without Frustration (Englewood Cliffs, N.J.: Prentice-Hall, 1983).

Sheehy, Gail
Passages: Predictable Crises of Adult Life (New York: Bantam Books, 1977).
Pathfinders (New York: Bantam Books, 1982).

Siropolis, Nicholas C.
Small Business Management: A Guide to Entrepreneurship (Boston: Houghton Mifflin, 1977). A remarkably good textbook.

Tepper, Terri and Nono
The New Entrepreneurs: Women Working from Home (New York: Universe Books, 1981). Interviews with women entrepreneurs.

Terkel, Studs
Working (New York: Pantheon Books, 1974). Enlightening interviews tell how most people feel about their work.

Toffler, Alvin
Future Shock (New York: Random House, 1970).
The Third Wave (New York: William Morrow, 1980).

Townsend, Robert
Up the Organization (New York: Knopf, 1970). Sane and sensible advice from an Avis executive.

SMALL BUSINESS ADMINISTRATION

Created by Congress in 1953, the Small Business Administration encourages, assists, and seeks to improve the lot of small business in the United States. The central office is located in Washington, D.C. Services are delivered through nearly a hundred field offices located in major cities.

Here are some of the services available. For more complete information contact a local SBA office in your area. Look under United States Government in the phone book.

Publications

To receive a full list of all SBA publications, request Publication 115A (free booklets) or 115B (for-sale booklets). Call 800-372-6412 or write:

> U.S. Small Business Administration
> P. O. Box 15434
> Fort Worth, TX 76119

Loan Guaranty Program

Regional SBA offices process loan applications. The following is an outline of information required to complete an SBA loan package.

   I. Summary—Business Operation and Loan Request
      A. Nature of business
      B. Amount of loan request
      C. Purpose of loan request
      D. Repayment terms
      E. Source of repayment
      F. Security or collateral available with itemized estimate of market value
  II. Personal Information (Owners and Management Team)
      A. Educational and business history
      B. Financial statement (not older than sixty days)
      C. Income tax returns (last three years)
      D. Credit references
 III. Firm Information for Existing Businesses
      A. Business history
      B. Balance sheet (current within the last sixty days *and* balance sheets for the past three to five years)
      C. Profit and loss statement (current within the last sixty days and for the last three to five years)
      D. Cash flow statement for last year
      E. Federal tax returns for the past three to five years
      F. Lease agreements and business permit data

IV. Insurance Program
V. Business Plan
   A. Summary
      1. Business description
        a. Name
        b. Location and plant description
        c. Product
        d. Market and competition
        e. Management expertise
      2. Business goals
      3. Summary of financial needs and application of funds
      4. Earnings projections and potential return to investors
   B. Market analysis
      1. Description of total market
      2. Industry trends
      3. Target market
      4. Competition
   C. Products or services
      1. Description of product line
      2. Proprietary position: patents, copyrights, legal and technical considerations
      3. Comparison to competitors' products
   D. Manufacturing process (if applicable)
      1. Materials
      2. Source of supply
      3. Production methods
   E. Marketing strategy
      1. Overall strategy
      2. Pricing policy
      3. Sales terms
      4. Method of selling, distributing, and servicing products
   F. Management plan
      1. Form of business organization
      2. Board of directors composition
      3. Officers: organization chart and responsibilities
      4. Résumés of key personnel
      5. Staffing plan/numbers of employees
      6. Facilities plan/planned capital improvements
      7. Operating plan/schedule of upcoming work for next one or two years
   G. Financial data
      1. Financial history (five years to present)
      2. Five-year financial projections (first year by quarter; remaining years annually)
        a. Profit and loss statements
        b. Balance sheets
        c. Cash flow chart
        d. Capital expenditure estimates

3. Explanation of projections
4. Key business ratios—current ratio, quick ratio, debt to net worth
5. Explanation of use and effect of new funds
6. Potential return to investors compared to competitors and the industry in general

VI. Projections
   A. Profit and loss projections (monthly for one year); explanation of basis for projections
   B. Cash flow projections (monthly for one year); explanation of basis for projections
   C. Projected balance sheet (at end of year); explanation of projections

Women-in-Business Representatives

The Small Business Administration has recently instructed each regional office to appoint an employee who is a special representative to women in business. Responsibilities vary from office to office. In some cases the women-in-business representative makes presentations to the community. This is called "outreach." In other cases the women-in-business representative functions as a special advocate in situations of disputes. Call your regional office for details on local programs.

SCORE

SCORE, the Service Corps of Retired Executives, is a volunteer group of retired men and women who provide free management counseling to small business owners and those who are considering starting a business. SCORE was developed by SBA in 1964 as a means of tapping the vast business expertise of the growing ranks of top-notch retired executives for the benefit of America's small business community.

Make contact with SCORE through SBA regional offices or your local Chamber of Commerce.

NON BANK LENDERS

In 1958, Congress passed the Small Business Investment Act. This allowed the formation of two types of lenders to small businesses that are *not banks*—small business investment companies and small business lending concerns.

Small Business Investment Companies

Small business investment companies are interested in increasing the flow of equity capital and long-term loan funds to small businesses.

That means that they are venture capitalists. They want to own a share of your business for the money they put in. They are generally interested in funding businesses based on high technology or ones that are likely to grow up fast to Fortune 500 status.

The SBICs are joined together in a national organization called the National Association of Small Business Investment Companies. To get a list of local members, write for their Membership Directory:

National Association of Small Business Investment Companies
618 Washington Building
Washington, DC 20005

Small Business Lending Concerns

If your business will have a slower, saner growth pattern and you qualify for an SBA loan guarantee, you might check into a small business lending concern.

Basically, an SBLC acts just like a bank. It makes you a loan, the loan is backed by an SBA guarantee, and you pay off the loan. Everyone is happy.

John Wagner, vice-president of The Money Store, an SBLC with offices in eight states, points out one huge advantage. "We're specialists in working with SBA guaranteed loans. Most banks are not. In fact, banks hate to do an SBA loan because of the paperwork. Doing this sort of loan is our one and sole activity. We are real pros. And we can get approval fast—generally in two weeks."

Working with an organization such as The Money Store, you get free consulting as a loan applicant. All the loan officers have experience with small business. And they want to make a good loan. They will question, probe, suggest changes, help you improve your business plan.

You can obtain a full list of these non bank lenders from:

Small Business Administration
Financial Assistance Division
Office of Lender Relations and Certifications
Non Bank Lender Section
Washington, DC 20416

COURSES

Courses in small business are available at all levels of the educational ladder. Take advantage of them! You will not only gather needed information, you will meet lots of interesting women.

Junior or Community Colleges

The National Small Business Training Network is comprised of 186 two-year colleges established and maintained through a grant from the Small Business Administration. They concentrate on getting you practical, affordable, high-quality training in forty-seven states. In the first half of 1982 nearly 40,000 people participated in entrepreneurial courses at local colleges.

Here is a sample:

"Business of Art and the Artist," Community College of Allegheny County in Pittsburgh, Pennsylvania; "Solvency Management and Bankruptcy Avoidance," El Paso Community College in El Paso, Texas; "Incorporating a Small Business," Tri County Technical College in Pendleton, South Carolina; "Independent Consulting: Is It for You?" Montgomery College in Rockville, Maryland; "Your Small Business Is Your Tax Shelter," Jackson Community College in Jackson, Mississippi; "Am I a Woman Entrepreneur?" Napa College in Napa, California.

Though few of these courses are directed specifically toward women, women generally make up about half of every class. The average age of class members, by the way, is thirty-five.

Generally courses run from six to ten weeks, cost fifty dollars or less, and are *not* taken for credit. Junior and community colleges also sponsor three- or four-hour short courses.

Get on your local college's mailing list and find out what's coming up.

Colleges and Universities

Colleges and universities tend to place more emphasis on management theory, courses for credit, and degree programs.

One of the outstanding university programs in entrepreneurship is the Center for Private Enterprise and Entrepreneurship at Baylor University, Waco, Texas. The program includes both an undergraduate concentration in entrepreneurial studies and a Master of Business Administration in Entrepreneurship and Venture Management degree.

An Innovation Evaluation Center offers a valuable service to inventors or designers of new products. For a seventy-five-dollar fee a team of business experts will evaluate your invention by thirty-three different criteria, which cover investment and market factors, promotion and distribution, price, and competition. For further information write:

> Innovation Evaluation Program
> Center for Private Enterprise and Entrepreneurship
> Hankamer School of Business
> Baylor University
> Waco, TX 76798

Hankamer School of Business also sponsors a Venture Assistance Program. Other universities have similar programs. Undergraduate or graduate students, under the direction of faculty members, act as small business management consultants for local businesses. Fees, if they exist, are minimal.

Call your local college or university to inquire whether they have a small business development and assistance center on campus.

ORGANIZATIONS, CLUBS, AND NEWSLETTERS

American Women's Economic Development Corporation

American Women's Economic Development Corporation provides entrepreneurial women with comprehensive business training, counseling, and technical assistance.

Founded in 1976 by Beatrice Fitzpatrick and located in New York City, AWED is dedicated to the idea that American women are the greatest single untapped resource in this country. The organization offers the following services.

Counseling sessions. Ninety-minute counseling sessions are available at the AWED New York office. Fee $25.

Telephone counseling. The same service is available by phone for women living outside the New York area. Fee $25.

Hotline. AWED will supply quick answers to urgent questions in a ten-minute phone session. Fee $5.00.

Courses. AWED offers two courses for women who run their own businesses. "How to Build Your Own Business" is a nine-session course designed for businesses that have survived the first birth pangs but are not ready for the course below. Fee $175.

"How to Manage Your Own Business" is a twenty-six-session course for women who have been in business at least six months and who are ready for advanced, sophisticated, intensive business training. Fee $350.

American Women's Economic Development Corporation
The Lincoln Building
60 East 42nd Street
New York, NY 10165
(212) 692-9100   (800) 222-AWED is their toll-free number

American Women Entrepreneurs

American Women Entrepreneurs is a national network of dedicated women helping one another achieve bigger and better business success. Low-cost group-rate insurance, product and service discounts, subscription to a national newsletter, referral to women business owners in other cities are some of the services available through the organization. Request additional information and application form from American Women's Economic Development Corporation in New York City. Annual membership fee $50.

National Alliance of Homebased Businesswomen

Until the founding of NAHB in 1981, women working from home could not belong to a professional organization. Many women who use their homes as business locations do not take themselves or their homebased businesses seriously. NAHB is solving that problem.

The organization publishes a quarterly newsletter, encourages the formation of local chapters, and works hard in Washington to lobby for legislation supporting homebased workers. Write for more information.

National Alliance of Homebased Businesswomen
P. O. Box 306
Midland Park, NJ 07432

National Association of Women Business Owners

NAWBO membership is composed of women engaged in almost every facet of American industry and commerce from advertising and public relations to towing and excavation. The organization is building a network of women in business to influence national policy, expand programs and public relations for women business owners, and working to ensure all women entrepreneurs a full partnership in the world of commerce.

NAWBO has a national headquarters in Chicago and chapters in twenty-five cities. Write for more information.

National Association of Women Business Owners
500 North Michigan Avenue
Chicago, IL 60611

Newsletter

To Market, to Market is a monthly newsletter published by Upstream Press, which simplifies complex marketing theories so they can be applied to small business operations. It is a practical how-to guide for getting your product or service to market. Each issue covers topics ranging from the strange behavior of people when they become sellers and buyers to detailed case studies of small business marketing plans that work. It is an invaluable aid to both women business owners who are just starting and those who wish to expand an existing business. Annual subscription, $36.00.

Upstream Press Inc.
P.O. Box 2033
Rohnert Park, CA 94928